Making Urban Bu

FOR MODEL RAILWAYS

Making Urban Buildings
FOR MODEL RAILWAYS

David Wright

THE CROWOOD PRESS

First published in 2013 by
The Crowood Press Ltd
Ramsbury, Marlborough
Wiltshire SN8 2HR

www.crowood.com

This impression 2017

British Library Cataloguing-in-Publication Data
A catalogue record for this book is available from the British Library.

ISBN 978 1 84797 568 3

Dedication
I would like to dedicate this, my second book, to a good friend and fellow modeller,
John Gaskin, who sadly passed away with prostate cancer while I was compiling it.

Disclaimer
The author and the publisher do not accept any responsibility in any manner
whatsoever for any error or omission, or any loss, damage, injury, adverse outcome
or liability of any kind incurred as a result of the use of any of the information
contained in this book, or reliance upon it.

Typeset by Servis Filmsetting Ltd, Stockport, Cheshire
Printed and bound in Malaysia by Times Offset (M) Sdn Bhd

CONTENTS

INTRODUCTION

Before we look at constructing models of urban buildings for your model railway, it is worth spending some time considering what you may realistically aspire to achieve and what will be physically possible. It is so easy to get carried away in attempting to build a model beyond the capability of one person. Before you start you should ask yourself:

- What spare time can I realistically allow myself to build the model?
- Do I have the physical space?
- Do I have the physical capability?
- Can I realistically afford the expense?
- Am I looking to build a true representation of an actual railway and location, or do I just want to run trains through an urban landscape without a specific authenticity?
- Will I achieve full satisfaction from building this model?

These questions are not intended to put you off, far from it, but it is important to ask them during the planning stage. So many model railways have been or never will be finished because this has not been addressed properly. By definition a model railway set in an urban scene will always lead to grand ideas to create something larger than one in a rural setting. It might, for example, be worth considering only a small urban station or leaving one out altogether. I will endeavour to cover this subject in detail in

Ivatt 2P 2-6-2 tank 41296 awaits to go onto the shed on the 7mm 'Wychnor-on-Trent' layout. Photo: John Hancock

The magnificent arch of the Iron Bridge, spanning the River Severn. The first cast iron bridge has become an enduring symbol of the birth of the Industrial Revolution. The valley is now a World Heritage site.

Chapter 4, where I will look at both planning and setting a model railway into the urban landscape.

As with all aspects of railway modelling, if we are hoping to build miniature versions of urban buildings it helps to have some knowledge of their history and the materials used to construct them.

In this book I will concentrate on urban development following the Industrial Revolution and up to the present day. This was a period of mass expansion and change that included the development of the railways and other forms of transport.

Close examination of a town will reveal the history of its development from an early nucleus around a market place or square. Before the Industrial

Ex. Midland Class 3F 43244 awaits its next turn of duty to shunt the brewery exchange sidings on the 'Wychnor' layout. Photo: John Hancock

LMS Class 4F 44558 returns on the the shed after working brewery traffic. Photo: John Hancock

Revolution, most were originally market towns that supplied all necessary trades to the surrounding rural areas. This economic model, however, was transformed during the eighteenth and nineteenth centuries. Abraham Darby's introduction of a coke smelting method in 1709 enabled him to manufacture pig iron of a higher quality and more cheaply than previously. He used deposits of local coal to produce coke to fuel the furnaces at Coalbrookdale in the gorge of the River Severn. The valley soon became a centre of mass production. The gorge today is a UNESCO World Heritage site with a collection of museums describing its industrial past, symbolized by the magnificent Iron Bridge erected in 1779, which spans the river with one enormous arch and gives its name to the complex.

Cromford Mill was the first successful water-powered cotton mill. It was here that Richard Arkwright pioneered the water frame in 1771, originating the factory system.

Water became the first source of power to operate the new mills and factories. The Industrial Revolution would see these occupying many of Britain's river valleys and turning them into centres of industry.

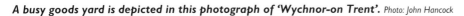

A busy goods yard is depicted in this photograph of 'Wychnor-on Trent'. *Photo: John Hancock*

The three-storey building in stone is the weavers' workshop at Cromford Mill. Here hand-loom workers were employed to work up the yarn. This building would make a very interesting subject for a model.

An industrial landscape is modelled to perfection. The photograph shows the goods and coal yards in the station area at 'Eccleston'. The layout is the work of Martin Nield. Photo: Martin Nield

Another textile mill along the banks of the River Derwent in Derbyshire was built by Thomas Evans at Darley Abbey to produce high-quality cotton thread. Pictured is the oldest building in the complex, the Long Mill, which dates from 1790. The wooden sash-window frames and 'X'-shaped tie-bar plates should both be noted. A new village was also constructed to house all the workers.

The impressive frontage of Richard Arkwright's Mason Mill, standing between Cromford and Matlock Bath. It was built from Accrington red brick set on gritstone foundations, with Venetian windows flanking a tier of lunettes. The bell tower was provided to call the workers in for the shift.

The Silk Mill on the banks of the River Derwent was the first factory in the country. Only the foundations and the tower survived a fire that destroyed the original eighteenth-century building, however, the building shown here is a smaller reconstruction that is now the home of Derby's Museum of Industry. The famous Midland Railway model exhibit is housed on the first floor and the author was responsible for constructing a good number of its buildings and structures.

The Industrial Revolution also saw the introduction and development of machinery for producing textiles, beginning with the Spinning Jenny developed by James Hargreaves. The water-powered spinning frames that Richard Arkwright installed in a mill at Cromford, Derbyshire, were closely followed by others using water power from the River Derwent. Like the Iron Bridge Gorge, the Derwent Valley has now been granted UNESCO World Heritage status.

The new industries required power to keep the machinery running. The first source was water and all the early mills were built along the course of a river to supply this. Later factories and mills would be powered by steam, which required the mining of large quantities of coal. The task of sinking deep pits for this was itself assisted by the development of steam-powered beam engines for draining the mines. With the pumps in place, deep mines started to appear in areas of the country with rich coal measures. Other minerals would be mined and quarried to provide the raw materials required. Coal and its by-products helped to fuel other industries and the mass production of goods from iron, copper, tin and steel. Besides the manufacturing industries, coal would be used for services and to process raw materials to produce food and drink products. This period would see the expansion of the brewing industry from a local activity to the creation of major breweries supplying beer to the world.

Alongside this rapid industrial expansion there was an immediate need to house all the people moving into the towns and cities to provide the essential labour. Most of the labour moved from the country, drawn by the promise of higher wages and a better standard of living. The Victorian era saw towns considerably enlarged as massive areas were covered with terrace rows of back-to-back houses, the most effective way of producing homes quickly for the ever growing population. In addition it was necessary to ensure services to educate, entertain and provide health services and provisions as well as to serve the religious beliefs of the workers and their families. These houses and services would require coal as a fuel to provide all the heating and cooking requirements.

All this industry and housing also required an improved transport system to bring in raw materials and distribute the finished products around the country and abroad. The late eighteenth century would see the construction of a canal network to transport these goods. The first railways were developed to serve the mines, but it was not long before this method of transport was established all over the country to carry both goods and passengers.

In this book I will look at how our urban towns and cities developed and take a detailed look at the various buildings belonging to this era. Both industrial buildings and domestic housing will be examined, together with buildings that were provided for services and transport. As we take a look at the prototypes, I will endeavour to describe how miniature versions can be constructed for our model railways.

A row of original weavers' cottages at Lea Mills, Derbyshire.

A Duchess rounds the curve and crosses the canal, drifting into 'Wychnor-on-Trent' station with an express from the north. Note how this corner of the layout has been filled with the industrial brewery cameos.

Photo: John Hancock

TOOLS AND MATERIALS

The following section provides guidance regarding the selection of tools, equipment and basic materials that you will need in order to build models of urban buildings as described in this book. For all the modelling techniques used, I would strongly recommend the wearing of safety glasses.

ABOVE: *When measuring large industrial buildings you will need to acquire the longest tape measures you can find. Short tapes are handy for measuring items such as the windows and doors.*

ABOVE: *While impact adhesives are fine for gluing most materials, they can dissolve some of the foam used in the core of foam board. When you are bonding foam board together it is better to use a universal polyvinyl acetate (uPVA) adhesive.*

ABOVE: *Bostik is an impact adhesive suitable for most of your modelling needs.*

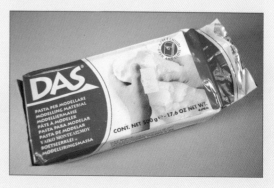

RIGHT: *Das modelling clay can be used to create a skin for any stone buildings or to fill gaps on other masonry where embossed styrene sheet has been used.*

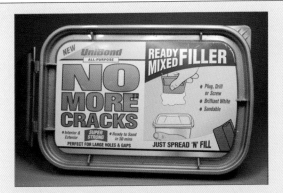

No More Cracks, a ready-mixed plaster filler made by Unibond, can be used to fill gaps and create rendered and pebble-dashed finishes.

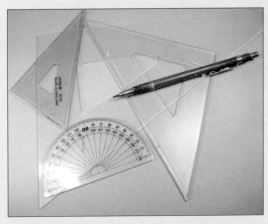

Some of the drawing equipment required to produce a working drawing.

Extra drawing equipment is needed to produce windows with arched or curved tops.

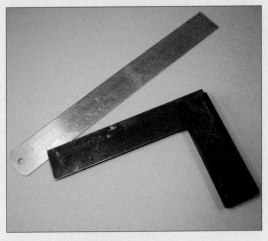

A short metal ruler and small square will come in handy for many stages of model making.

Good quality double-sided tape can be used as a cleaner alternative to glue when fixing slates and roof tiles.

An embossing tool can be used to produce bolt and rivet heads on door hinges and for riveted plates on water tanks, oil tanks and gas holders.

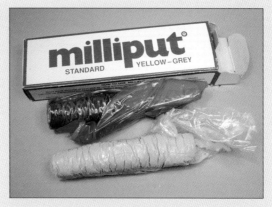

Milliput epoxy putty is used as a filler and to create the flaunching holding the chimney pots to the stack.

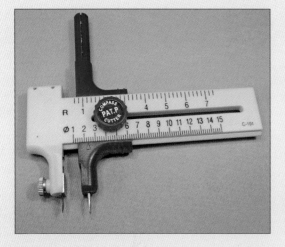

A compass cutter comes in handy when cutting arched or curved window apertures.

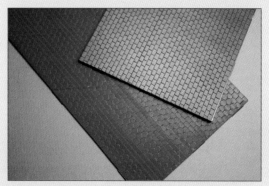

Embossed plastic building sheets from the Wills range.

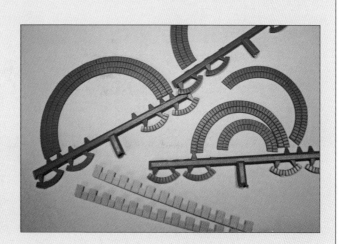

Wills corner quoins and brick arched lintels.

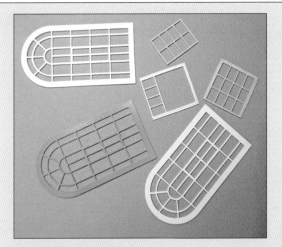

A selection of laser-cut industrial window frames from York Modelmaking.

Industrial metal-framed windows with centre-pivoted opening lights. These were commissioned to be etched from drawings by GT Models.

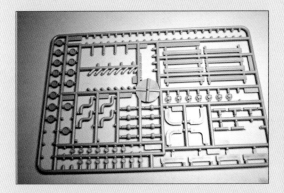

Plastic pipes and valves, such as these supplied by Knightwing, will come in handy when modelling a gasworks or brewery.

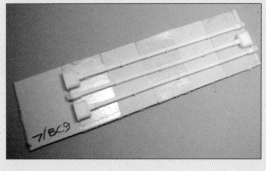

Square-profiled downpipes with hoppers produced in resin for 7mm scale by Skytrex Models.

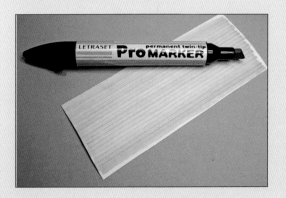

The results of scribing planking on card and then adding the colour by using a Pro-marker pen.

CHAPTER ONE

INDUSTRIAL BUILDINGS

In this chapter I will look at some of Britain's first industrial buildings as well as those from later periods. The first factories were textile mills. Initially the machinery was powered by water, but this was eventually superseded by steam and finally electricity. Mills became a common feature of the urban landscape, especially in the northern counties of Derbyshire, Yorkshire and Lancashire, although they could be found elsewhere: mills for processing wool, for example, were built in the Cotswolds (Stroud, Chipping Norton and Bradford-on-Avon) and in Devon (Buckfastleigh).

The building materials used varied depending on the local area, although brick and stone were the most common. The outer load-bearing walls were of substantial construction in order to support all the

Cauldwell's Mill is an example of an industrial building built from gritstone. Note the square metal-framed, multi-paned windows and the weathering around the downpipe.

An Aspinall 0-6-0 Saddle Tank locomotive shunts the Vegetable Warehouse on Martin Nield's pre-grouping L&YR layout, 'Eccleston'. The warehouse was built by Andy Thompson and is based on photographs of a prototype in Burscough, Lancashire.

The extensive Ryknild Mills complex in the West End area of Derby. Note how many multi-paned, iron-framed windows are fitted to each floor, a common feature of this type of building.

The 1804 North Mill at Belper, Derbyshire, was designed to a 'T'-plan footprint by William Strutt. The Strutt family introduced the textile industry to Belper using power provided by the River Derwent. Like Thomas Evans at Darley Abbey, the Strutts provided housing, farms and schools for all their mill workers.

The road elevation of Arkwright's stone-built Bakewell Mill. Windows are inserted only in the first two storeys. The top floor and attic are lit only by deep windows set in the gable ends.

The Long Mill at Darley Abbey Mills, built by Thomas Evans in 1782, was rebuilt after a fire in 1790. This brick rectangular building, with five storeys, had a schoolroom in the attic to provide a basic education for children working at the mill.

high-rise floors. Ditherington Flax Mill in Shrewsbury has a claim to be the world's first completely iron-framed building; this design transferred the load to the iron frame, allowing the walls to be built from a thinner masonry. This innovation was to pave the way for the eventual development of skyscrapers. The multi-storeyed mill and factory buildings were built with wide and long open floors, supported by cast iron pillars from the floor below, to house the textile machinery. The walls would have a repeated pattern of windows to allow as much daylight as possible onto the operating floors. This floor layout was to become the common practice in textile mills, maltings, factories and warehouses.

The early mills had wooden windows of a casement or sash design. Later buildings used the new materials of cast iron and steel. The windows featured multi-paned glazing panels with an opening light either hinged at the top or centre pivoted. These designs could be square, rectangular or often with an arched fanlight top.

The roofs were supported on a series of wooden trusses constructed in either a gabled or hipped style. Later mills and factories would adopt the saw-toothed roof design known as 'North Lights', which used a series of lighter frame trusses made from timber or, later, steel. This design allowed for the steeper profile to be glazed, giving optimal daylight

to penetrate onto the work floor. The roofs would also feature ventilation systems. Glazing panels offered opening lights. Extra ventilation systems were added to the roof space, especially in factories, including fans to take out the stale, contaminated air and replace it with fresh air. Most of these ventilators used a cylindrical pattern with a fan mounted horizontally within.

The first mills and factories were powered by a water supply directed to spin a wheel. This would be connected to the main drive shaft, to which all the machinery was connected by a series of wheels and belts. Steam power was soon adapted to power the mills and factories, requiring an engine and boiler house to be added to existing buildings or built within newer structures. This would see the urban skyline punctuated with tall stone and brick chimneys.

For more than two centuries the textile mills and factories dominated urban life in the north. Change came with cheaper imports of textiles. From the 1960s these imposing buildings began to disappear and one by one the mill chimneys were brought crashing to the ground. New methods of manufacture using ever developing technology required different factory building types. Prefabricated steel-framed units clad with corrugated steel panels would become the standard form of construction, with the buildings grouped together on special sites. Modern

A typical stone mill chimney. Note the octagonal shape with decorative rim and the expansion steel bands fixed along the barrel.

factory units on industrial estates are clean and functional, using developing technology to substitute for labour.

CREATING SCALE MODELS

In order to make convincing and accurate scale models of industrial buildings, you first need to do your research and then reproduce this in practical ways.

MEASUREMENTS

With any model there will be a need to gather information, either by visiting the site or from photographs. You should start with the measurements. For large buildings, such as industrial mills and factories, these will have to be estimated. One way of estimating the height of a building is by counting the masonry courses. This is only possible, though, if the building is constructed from regular-sized stone courses or brick. The lengths can be measured at ground level using a tape, include the dimensions of any ground-floor windows and doors. Windows in the upper floors will usually repeat those of the ground floor, so their sizes and position should be reasonably easy to calculate. It is generally impossible to measure the rooflines of these large buildings with a tape, as access can be very awkward. It can also be a huge problem estimating structures such as a mill chimney, although it is possible to make a start with a window or door (always a good starting point). It is then a matter of visual scaling from the dimensions you know to estimate these awkward measurements. Make a rough sketch of the building, including all the dominant features, and add all the measurements taken to this.

The tall, round, brick-built mill chimney of Arkwright's Mason Mill. Note the square flue base and decorative fluting to the top.

How to estimate some of the measurements needed to make a model. Take a photograph of the front elevation of the mill, trying to keep the angles as straight as possible. Lines are then drawn over the print with the measurements marked on. This is achieved by estimating the size of one window and basing the other measurements on this.

Another way is to photograph your prototype from the sides and ends from a reasonable distance, trying to keep the walls straight and vertical. Lay a sheet of tracing paper over the printed photograph or you could mark on it directly. Draw over the section for which you have a good idea of the measurements, such as a door or window, and then trace or mark on other lines over the rest of the building. This will enable you to build up a good idea of the other measurements.

PHOTOGRAPHY

I would always recommend taking as many photographs of the prototype as possible, in addition to those made for estimating measurements. Take three-quarter views and plenty of close-up images of all the features and details. It will be a good idea to make photographic notes of colour variations within the masonry and roof covering, observing where and how the building has been affected by the weather.

DRAWINGS AND MOCK-UPS

Once you have gathered all the information together for your model you will need to prepare a drawing to the desired scale. Take your time. I always use a drawing board, using the parallel motion fitted to the board to create the horizontal lines and a set square to draw the verticals. You will also require a hard lead pencil, or drawing pen, such as those

Cardboard mock-up of a large flour mill, with photocopies taken from the drawings cut and pasted onto the walls. I would always recommend making a mock-up such as this before constructing the model, since this will give you an impression of how the building will fit into its surroundings.

available as fibre tips from the likes of Edding, Pilot and Staedtler. You can use a compass or circle template for windows with round tops or arches. An eraser might be handy to have in case of any mistakes, and a scale rule for whatever scale you are working to. If you have relevant drawing software it could be originated on the computer and then printed out, but working to model scales might prove to be a problem for some computer programs and I prefer to use the old-fashioned methods to prepare all my drawings.

When you have completed drawings of all the elevations or sides that will be visible, make a series of photocopies. These can be used to create a mock-up by pasting or spray mounting them onto carton cardboard. Once mounted the elevations are cut out and assembled to make a three-dimensional mock-up of the building. The mock-up will be a considerable help in determining the finished model. Another advantage is that it can be placed on the baseboard, giving you a good idea of how the finished model will appear in relation to its immediate surroundings and the extent to which it might dominate the scene. This will always be more important when fitting a large building such as a mill into your model railway.

MATERIALS AND ASSEMBLY

The drawing can now be transferred over to the modelling material. For the mill to be built I would

recommend using mounting board, which is available from arts and crafts suppliers and is used mainly by picture framers. This material has been chosen as, besides being strong, it will be easy to cut out all those windows. Handling will be easier if you cut out the window and door apertures, using a scalpel or hobby knife with a sharp blade, before cutting out the elevations. Add an extra 10mm to the bottom of the elevations to give the mill some footings. This will also make life easier when it comes to painting the model, and of course will allow the models to fit into the surface of the base board.

Before assembling the cut-out elevations, the walls need to be covered with a material to replicate brick or stone masonry. A skin of Das modelling clay could be applied, but I would use this on a building of this size only if the stone masonry was irregular coursed or rubble stone. Das clay would also be applied once the walls of the building had been assembled together and sufficient corner and stretcher bracing added. The coursing could then be scribed out replicating the specific stonework of the prototype. If the mill is built from brick or a regular-coursed stone, however, I would choose to use a pre-embossed styrene sheet material, such as those produced by Slater's Plastikard.

The next stage is to fix the pre-scribed styrene sheet to the card, making sure that the coursing is level and lines up on the unassembled walls. It might be worth drawing a few lines along the length, about five courses apart, to act as a guide when ensuring that everything is perfectly level all the way around when the walls are assembled together. The sheets will need to overlap the card underneath on the side walls only by about 2mm. The sheets can now be fixed to the face of the card using glue

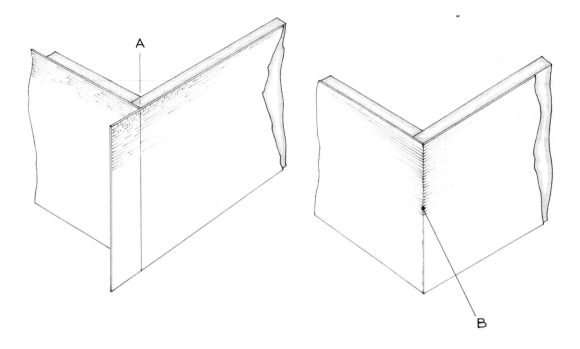

How to create a join using embossed styrene brick sheet: (A) one sheet has first been glued on to the building's shell, overlapping the other. When fixing the sheets it is important to ensure that the coursing lines up on all the sides and continues around the corner. (B) At the corner the overlapping section is cut square along the edge to make a neat butt joint. A small amount of filler can be added to the joint before extending the mortar courses around the corner using a fine needle file.

Double-sided tape is an alternative means of fixing embossed styrene sheet to the card shell of the building.

Fix the strips of double-sided tape to the card shell and then peel the backing paper away.

The embossed brick styrene sheet can now be fixed cleanly to the card shell, avoiding any unsightly bumps that sometimes accrue when using glue.

Cutting the card back by 5mm to leave a lip of the facing styrene will create a neater corner.

The lip is clearly shown here. When cutting the card be very careful not to cut through the styrene sheet as well.

When the two walls come together at the corner, note how one side has the extended lip of styrene sheet and the other is cut off flush.

Once the corner has been glued and secured, cut off the surplus styrene to create a clean butt joint.

The corner should now look like this, with a neat join and the coursing lining up around the corner.

Clean up using fine sandpaper to finish off the joint.

The coursing can be extended around the corner using a needle or fine file.

The finished corner to the brick wall.

or double-sided tape. Once you are happy that the coursing is level, the window apertures should be cut out on the styrene sheet material. The easiest way is to cut first diagonally, across the corners, then cut along the sides, top and bottom. This way the styrene should come away cleanly at the corners.

Once all the windows and doors have been cut out, add any corner quoins, lintels and sills that the building might need. These are cut from thicker styrene sheet; the quoins are also scored. Curved and arched lintels can be cut from plain sheet or parallel pre-grooved sheet, which needs to be cut out square into a strip, with the grooves vertical, at right angles to the cut. To create the curve, cut into the groove with the tip of the blade, starting at the top, but make sure the cut is only halfway into the depth of the lintel. With all the grooves cut in this way the strip of styrene can be gently curved.

The window frames can now be fitted into the cut-out apertures. On the prototype frames these will be made from either wood or metal, usually with multiple panes. Those made from timber will be of the casement and sash style, while the metal frames consist of a multiple-paned panel with an opening light. To model a mill, numerous window frames will be required of the same size and style. I would recommend having them etched from brass sheet, especially for the metal types and if your model is to be 4mm scale or less. For 7mm and larger scales the frames could be laser cut. Both methods require a scale drawing as an original master. If you are confident in your skills, try drawing the master at twice the scale size as this will make things a little easier. The operator can then reduce it to the correct size when producing the etchings or laser cuts. If you are not confident with producing a drawing, however, send a good quality photograph of the prototype window frame taken straight on. The processor will be able to convert this photograph into the master to use for etching or laser cutting, although this service will be added to the cost.

A little preparation will be needed before fitting the window frames into position in the pre-cut apertures. The window frames will require painting to match your prototype. I would recommend using spray paint for this, applying a spray primer first before spraying on the top coat. The glazing, made from a reasonable thickness of clear celluloid sheet, can now be fixed to the back of the frames. This

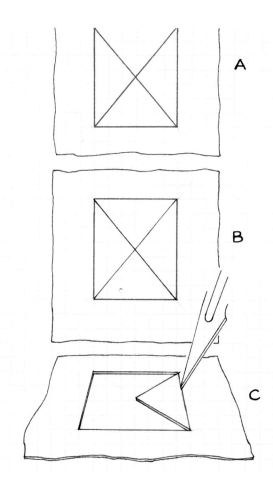

Cutting a window aperture out of the embossed styrene sheet on the face of the shell: (A) mark across the corners with a diagonal line; (B) cut along the diagonal lines using a sharp scalpel or hobby knife, always starting with a series of cuts before cutting all the way through; (C) cut the sides away up to the corners. Cutting diagonally first makes the corners come away more easily and gives a neater finish. The sides and corners will also require cleaning up, using the needle file to finish.

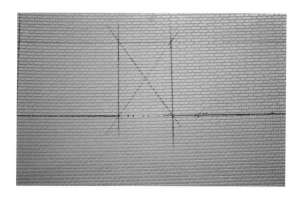

Marking out a window aperture onto the embossed styrene sheet.

Note how the diagonals are marked across the corners.

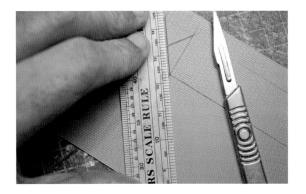

The first cut is along the diagonals into the four corners.

Once the diagonals have been cut, move on to cutting out the sides of the window, starting at the bottom.

Cutting the sides and the top. This method will give cleaner corners to the aperture.

The finished aperture.

The final stage is to clean up the edges and corners using a fine square file.

can often come from recycling clear packaging that would otherwise go in the bin. The film is cut out oversize. Spray mount is applied on the inside of the etched or laser-cut frame and this is then positioned on the clear celluloid film. When the bond has dried completely, trim the excess film away, leaving about 6mm all around the frame that can be used to fix the window into the aperture. The windows can then be fixed to the inside of the building's shell using glue, although a cleaner result will be obtained by using double-sided tape.

Once the windows are all in place, fix the doors into position before the sides are assembled

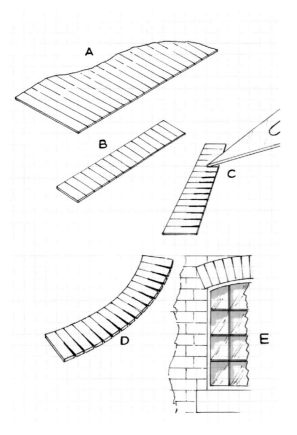

LEFT: *Cutting curved and arched segmental brick lintels: (A) start with a sheet of horizontal 2mm pre-embossed styrene; (B) cut a strip from the sheet to the width of the lintel; (C) cut along the groove to just over half the length, using the tip of a scalpel blade; (D) the strip can now be gently curved as required; (E) the finished curved lintel fitted and cut in to the wall above the window.*

BELOW: *Making doors: (A) The planking is scribed onto a sheet of card or Plastikard. Once the planks have been scored to the desired width, run the tip of the scalpel blade along the scored lines to create a 'V' groove. (B) Assembling the layers required to make up the door: 1. The plank-scribed door fits at the back, with enough left over at the sides and top to fix it to the frame. 2. The frame aperture is now fixed to the door with a weatherboard fitted to the bottom. 3. The final layer is the wall, with the cut-out aperture, which should be cut wider than the frame. (C) The final assembly of the door with the frame layer set back behind the (shaded) wall. Panelled doors are also assembled using the same process and order of assembly.*

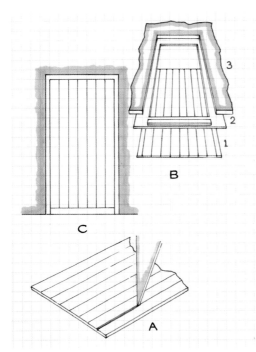

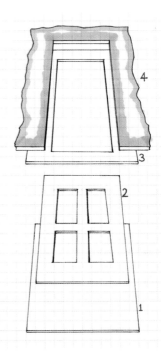

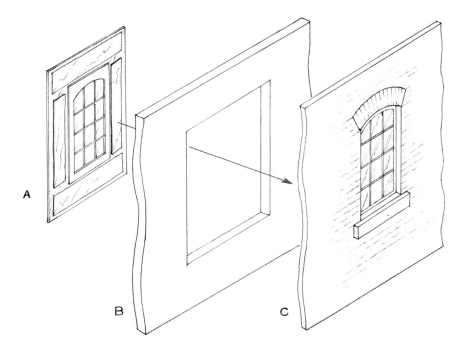

Fitting an industrial-etched or laser-cut window frame: (A) The frame is spray mounted onto the glazing material, which has been cut oversize. Strips of double-sided tape are then added to the sides, top and bottom. (B) An oversized aperture is cut in the inner card shell of the building to allow the window to pass through, complete with glazing. (C) The window in its final position fixed to the outer shell using double-sided tape to give the shallow reveals required.

Iron-framed windows were commonly fitted in most mills and industrial buildings. These were usually multi-paned with top or centre opening lights, either top-hinged or centre-pivoted. The frames also featured arched or curved tops.

Another sample of this type of industrial window, clearly showing the curve to the top of the frame.

together. Doors can be fabricated from thin card sheet or Plastikard. Use separate layers of card to make the door and door frame. For any panelled doors an extra layer will be required. Vertical planking can be achieved by scoring the planks onto the card's face or using one of the many available sheets of pre-grooved Plastikard. As with the windows, leave an overlap on the furthest back layer of card so that it can be fixed to the inside of the building's shell.

The wall sections can now be assembled together using square balsa wood strip to create a corner brace. Stretcher bracing will also be required, especially on a large building. Card strip or balsa wood can again be used for this, making sure that enough has been added to keep the building square. If the building sits on a plinth or has string courses, parapets or copings, these can now be added to the walls, perhaps by applying embossed stone or brick sheet.

Once the walls have been assembled the attention turns to the building's corners. Using the embossed sheet, all the courses will now need extending around each corner. If the sheet was put on correctly all the courses should line up. The reason for the overlap will now become apparent. The excess styrene sheet can be trimmed off level to create a butt joint at the corner. The next stage needs a reasonable amount of attention. Use a needle file to follow the coursing around the actual corner. Filing and cutting of the styrene can cause the plastic to feather and this will need to be cleaned up using a fine brass-bristled suede wire brush or fine sandpaper. This may take a considerable time to carry out as all the corners will need to be treated in this way. A small amount of filler plaster may be required to finish off the corner. This will need to be lightly sanded down again when dry to give the completed corner. If the corner has stone quoins these will have to be added. Depending on the size, these can be cut from styrene sheet or you might be able to utilize building accessories available from Wills Kits.

Once the walls are completely assembled, the roof can now be tackled. If the building has gable end walls, support strips will need to be fixed to the inside walls.

As these might not be enough to support a roof of this length, however, it might be a good idea to construct intermediate supports as roof trusses, which should be 'cut in' and fixed to the walls. The number of trusses will depend on the length of the building. Mills in which all the walls are the same size will have a hipped roof, or sometimes a series of hipped roofs. The latter would be supported on a series of cast iron or steel pillars running all the way through the building, supporting all the floors and finally the roof.

A Barton Wright 0-6-0 shunts wagons in front of the cotton mill at Eccleston, on Martin Nield's pre-grouping L&YR layout. The cotton mill is a mock-up, based on one in Preston, and will be replaced by a proper building in due course.

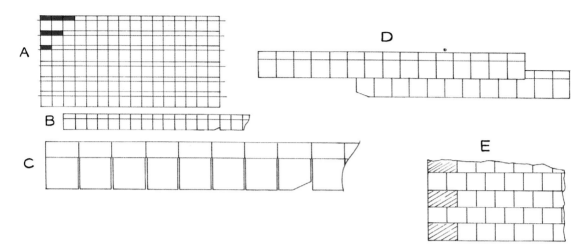

Cutting slates and tiles from card sheet. (A) First mark up the card. The red line indicates the overlap required between each row, which here needs to be about a third. The next black line will be cut through to make a strip of slates or tiles. (B) Once the strip has been cut, the next stage is to cut along each slate or tile up to the red overlap line. (C) Close-up showing how the occasional slate or tile has been cut at a shallow angle to replicate a broken edge. (D) The rows need to be overlapped to create the slate-covered or tiled roof. (E) The finished pattern. The shaded area demonstrates a one-and-a-half width tile, which were often added to alternate rows to avoid the possibility of wind damage to the edge of the roof.

The hipped roof for the model can be constructed by using a series of trusses for a single span roof. The multiple spans will require a base fixing first across the top of the walls. The roofs can then be constructed in the same way as the single span.

The completed roof superstructure will require a covering, which for a mill would most commonly be of slates or tiles. The roof covering would be both well supported and well maintained during its working life. Slates can be cut from cartridge paper, while for tiles you can use thin card. The first process is to mark out the slates or tiles on the materials as a grid or use a pre-printed grid. Start by cutting halfway along the vertical grid lines up to the first horizontal line. This is to create the individual slates or tiles. Move up to the next horizontal line and cut all the way along it to produce a strip. Once the strips have been cut, they can be fixed to the sub-base of the roof; the strips will need to overlap on each row to create the all-over pattern.

Ridge tiles should now be added to finish the roof and any joins may need flashings to create a water-proof join. The ridge tiles can be made from folded card, with strips added to represent the joining flanges. For flashings, try using thin metal foil, which can be glued and burnished over the join and roofing material, as with the real thing. Other additions to the roof can include ventilators and sky lights.

FACTORIES

When making models of factories, most of the techniques and materials will be the same as those described above for making models of mills. Factories have a number of different features that also apply to the later mills.

A style commonly used for all types of factories, from textiles to engineering, was the single-floored building with a saw-toothed roof. These often had a steel frame with walls of brick or stone. In later buildings the walls tended to be prefabricated panels of corrugated steel or asbestos sitting on a plinth wall of brick.

I have already described how to reproduce solid walls from brick or stone. Other materials used on

The office bridge at the John Smedley Limited textiles factory clearly shows the date of 1784, making this one of the earliest factories in the country.

the prototypes can be fabricated from embossed styrene sheets, available from the likes of Evergreen, Slater's and the Wills Finecast building materials packs. The wall sections in this case could be fixed to a styrene strip frame, replicating the steel fabricated framework of the prototype. The plinth wall can be made from card, styrene or balsa wood, covered with embossed styrene sheet to represent the brick, stone or concrete blocks. Buildings with a solid expanse of walling would have the same window designs as those used for the mills. In those with prefabricated sides, however, glazing was often supplied by using large panels of glass. These would either consist of multiple panes in metal frames with opening lights, or of larger vertical panes held again by metal frames. This method introduced a good amount of natural light to the work floor. The glazing panels themselves were more generally frosted than clear. When it comes to modelling large sections of multiple panes, I would recommend the etched or laser-cut approach. The later style could be made in the same way or by making up the panels with the framework fixed directly onto the glazing material. To replicate the diffused effect produced by frosted glass panes, I use tracing paper or drafting film, spray mounted to the reverse side of the glazing sheet. Another way of creating this effect is to spray a light grey coating of paint, again onto the inside. Wall panels clad in the corrugated covering often used glazing panels made from semi-clear

corrugated materials such as uPVC or fibre glass. Pre-made styrene sheets for this are available in the Wills Finecast sheet range and from other suppliers. Alternative forms of ventilation need to be provided for factory buildings that adopt this design of glazing and ventilation panels, sometimes with fans, added near the top of the wall.

This view of a factory at Mason Mill clearly shows the 'North Lights' or saw-toothed design of its roof.

A close-up of the Mason Mill roof shows in detail the frosted glass panels used to glaze the north lights. The ridge has been finished with blue flanged ridge tiles and blue slates.

The shallow-pitched side of a saw-toothed roof would usually have a covering of slates or other material, such as corrugated metal, asbestos or even felting. The steeper, or sometimes vertical, pitched side would usually be glazed to allow extra daylight onto the working floor below. All these roofs would be supported on a framework of light timber or steel. The technique to model this uses the same process and materials as described above for prefabricated wall sections. The roof should be supported on strips added to the edge of the profiles to the walls. Wrap-over strips or flashings are added to make the roof ridge. The valleys between the individual roof sections again require waterproofing to form gutters; the rainwater would then be taken away with a downpipe. With such a large amount of water dispersed over a large area, the downpipe would probably require a rain hopper to be fitted at the head. Downpipes can be modelled by using brass or styrene rod, although you might be able to find pipes and hoppers available as white metal or plastic accessory parts from Langley, Wills and Ratio Models in 4mm scale, and from Skytrex and S&D Models in 7mm.

Roofs of this type will also be fitted with roof ventilators. Different styles are to be found, including cylindrical, linear and mushroom types, all with hoods. Skytrex Models produces a range of common

types in both 7mm and 4mm scale; these are ideal accessories for the scratch builder. Later factory buildings also feature air conditioning systems and air ducting might be added to the outside roof area.

Modern factories are compact units, usually built on special industrial estates using a series of combined steel girder wall and roof trusses positioned and bolted to anchor plates on the foundations. Metal stretcher beams link the trusses together; these will support cladding sheets to cover the roof and the walls. A plinth is built up around the building using blocks with a brick facing. Prefabricated structures of this type can be built in single or multiple units side by side. A prefabricated brick and block-built office

Two fabricated steel designs of ventilators.

Different styles and sizes of ventilators used on the Rolls-Royce factory roofs at Nightingale Road, Derby.

This factory roof in Burton-on-Trent has a ventilator fitted with a cowl top, together with a wind vane, to take the fumes away.

The roof and walls of this factory building in Burton upon Trent were completely clad with asbestos sheets. Note the round fan ventilators positioned in the top of the gable ends.

A panel of frosted glass roof lights seen in the slate-clad roof at the John Smedley Limited textiles factory.

The valley created where two roofs meet. The waterproofing used at this join is clearly shown, as is the slate used to cover this roof and the glazing panels.

Prefabricated factory office block fronts, such as here at Kerry Foods in Burton upon Trent, are a common sight at factories all over the UK.

Oil is used to heat and power most of our factories. The oil storage tanks shown here provided fuel for the boilers at John Smedley Limited.

block is usually to be found added to the side or the end of the factory unit.

An important feature of most early factory and mill buildings would be the addition of a boiler house, complete with a chimney, to provide steam to power a stationary steam engine, which in turn would work all the machinery. The steam would also provide heating to the buildings. In later years boilers were often converted to be fuelled by oil. Eventually electricity superseded these as the main source of power and the boiler house became redundant.

The boiler house can either be attached to the main factory or built separately, in which situation external pipes would be provided to link the two together. To model these, both the techniques and materials used need to match those employed for the factory and mill buildings. A building or some sort of a cover would be needed to store the solid fuel required, as well as a tank to hold a water supply. Later oil-fired boilers would require oil storage tanks situated alongside. Models of water and oil tanks, and any external pipework, are readily available. Ratio Models, for example, provides water and oil tanks and industrial fittings, as well as a steel chimney complete with a cowl and support wires. These are handy kits for any industrial modeller. Skytrex offers

The loading bay of a modern factory unit in Burton, built using a steel frame clad with a brick skin at the bottom and corrugated steel higher up and for the roof.

an excellent kit of a complete boiler house with a square chimney. At present this is only available in 7mm scale, but a 4mm version may follow.

Kits of water tanks that can be adapted may be had from Airfix (now marketed by Dapol). Knightwing provides accessory packs of external pipework complete with valves, bends and joining collars. Oil tanks and hoppers are also available, together with catwalks and external industrial staircases.

Close-up of the corner of a factory showing the use of two different cladding materials: steel corrugated panels on the sides and ends of the building and corrugated asbestos to clad the roof.

A factory chimney is a familiar sight. Until the mid-twentieth century most factories were both powered and heated by steam, all created by boilers burning coal. Each boiler house would require a tall chimney to take away the smoke produced. This stack, now redundant, was provided for the boilers at Egginton Dairy.

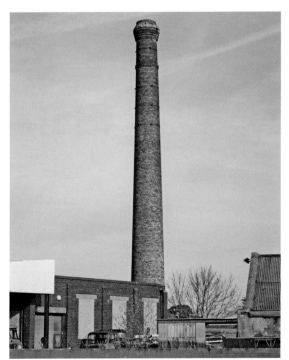

The office block to the original Rolls-Royce factory on Nightingale Road in Derby featured a facade and parapet decorated with a reed-moulded frieze. This decoration was very popular during the Art Deco period.

The impressive centrepiece to the Rolls-Royce factory was remodelled in 1938 by architects Arthur Easton & Son. The Art Deco masterpiece in Portland stone and steel was known as the Marble Hall owing to its lavish interior. It has a marble staircase and a wonderful arched stained glass window dedicated to the airmen who fought in the Battle of Britain. Today, however, the building is boarded up and its future is uncertain.

This model of Shirebrook Diesel Depot is included here as the prefabricated construction and cladding used on the main shed is similar to that on any modern factory unit. Note the ventilators fitted to the roof. The layout of the building is also representative of a modern factory with the office block located at the front.
Photo: Peter Grundel

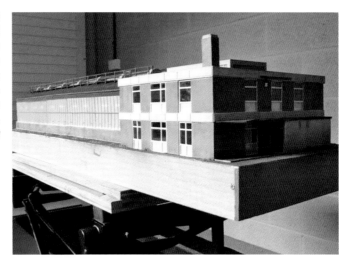

A close-up of the Shirebrook office block. The pre-fabricated panels of brick are fitted with floor-to-ceiling window panels. The first floor and roof have a concrete fascia and the roof is fitted with a pre-stressed concrete lantern top to allow more light into the building. Photo: Peter Grundel

Kits of other buildings or parts of buildings can also be utilized to create a boiler house or even the main factory. Take a look, for example, at the provender goods store, engine shed and carriage shed from Ratio Models, which also offers a coal/builders' merchants kit that would make a very good coal or coke store for any factory boiler house with only a few alterations, if any. The two-road engine shed kit from Wills Finecast, complete with its saw-toothed roof design, can be remodelled to make a very good factory of this period. The single-road engine shed, with attached water tank and louvre roof ventilator, could make a convincing boiler house, again with just a few additions or alterations. Metcalfe Models and, from the past, Bilt-eezi have both produced a total boiler complex including the chimney, as well as kits of complete factories, but these kits were only available in flat printed card and lack the relief of stone or brick masonry.

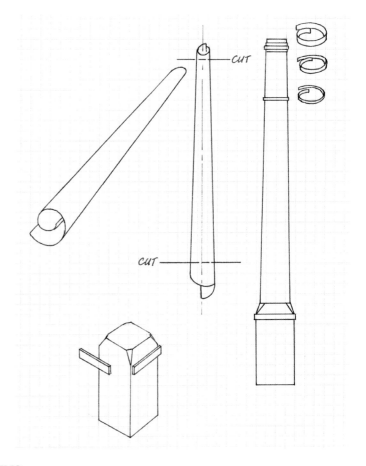

FACTORY AND MILL CHIMNEYS

Chimneys were a major feature of early factories and mills and merit some attention, although I will also look at the later steel fabricated stacks that are now more familiar.

Mill and factory chimneys were constructed from both stone and brick, usually built on a square plinth to create the base for the flue. The barrel of the chimney could then be found in a variation of profiles from square or octagonal to round.

There are a few kits or off-the-shelf models of chimneys on the market, such as the resin kits in 7mm scale from Skytrex and Invertrain Model Railways; these are of brick construction and are to a square profile. A plastic kit of a brick chimney with a round profile is available from Faller.

To build a factory or mill chimney from scratch, start with the square flue base. This can be fabricated from Plastikard, card or even wood and then be faced

A round stack chimney can easily be made from thin card. Roll the card at a slight angle to create the taper, glue the join and then cut off the top and bottom of the stack square. Add the projected string-coursed rim details and coat with layers of PVA to make the assembly more ridged. A final coat of PVA can be added, pre-mixed with some ready-mixed plaster. This will give the chimney the texture of brick or even concrete. The round stack can now be fitted up to a square flue base if required. This can be fabricated from mounting board and then coated with the plaster mix. It would be very difficult to scribe brick or stone coursing onto this structure, so I would advise trying to achieve this effect at the painting stage. If done well this can look very convincing, especially in the smaller scales.

The master for the new resin cast round chimney stack produced by 'Skytrex Model' for their 4mm range. The author was responsible for creating the master, all the brick work being scribed out by hand.

with embossed styrene brick or stone. If the profile of the chimney is square or octagonal the barrel can be made from the same materials, but a round profile chimney will require a different approach. The round barrel can either be rolled from thin card or it can be turned in wood on a lathe. The barrel of most round stacks will taper from a larger diameter at the base to a smaller diameter at the top. Both card and wood barrels require a skin of plaster filler brushed on and then all the brick or stone coursing scribed out. This is quite a daunting task, but it is worth it. Chimneys of this type usually had a series of plinths or cornice, combined with raised stringcourses, to make a decorative top just before the rim. This can be modelled by cutting a series of various sizes of card discs using a compass cutter. The stringcourse is made by wrapping a thin strip of paper or masking tape around the barrel about an inch from the top. These can then all be assembled together at the top of the barrel. To finish the job, use a section of card or styrene tube to create the top and rim to the chimney.

Modern chimneys are far simpler. Concrete stacks can still be tapered, but most steel and alloy stacks are parallel from the base up to the top. These can be modelled by using card, styrene or brass and aluminium tube, which is available from model material suppliers such as Eileen's Emporium.

The basic low relief panel of the Skytrex resin-cast 'North Lights' factory. This has been made modular so that more panels can be fitted together to make a longer building. The casting may require cleaning up to remove any flash, especially around the glazing bars.

The next stage is to spray on a coat of red primer to give the building a basic brick colour.

When the primer is dry, mix up a wash of oil paint using about 20 per cent Naples Yellow mixed with 80 per cent Titanium White. Combine this with lots of turpentine thinners to give the thin consistency required and brush this all over, allowing the thinned-down paint to run into all the mortar joints.

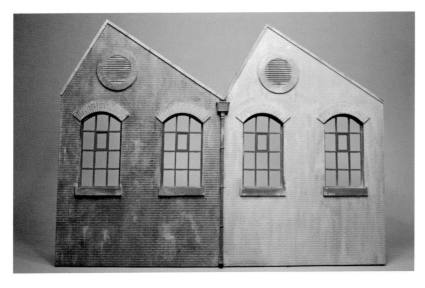

With the pre-sprayed brick colour exposed, take the wash colour off the surface by gently wiping with a paper towel. After leaving this to dry, you can start the process of dry-brushing paint onto the raised surface of the bricks.

The results of dry brushing the colour onto the brick work. Weathering and grime has also been added to create a realistic effect. (For a full description of dry brushing, see Chapter 5). The windows, ventilator louvres and drainpipe are all picked out in dark green, before a slight weathering finish is applied.

This modern factory gable end elevation, complete with loading bay door, is also from the Skytrex low relief range. As with the north light casting, more can be added if required.

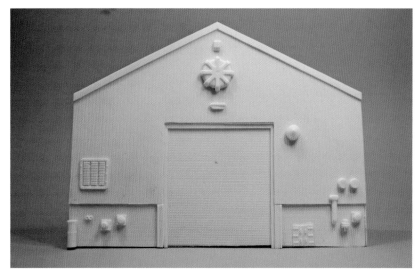

Before moving on it is worth looking at some of the models of factories that are available off the shelf. There are good examples of both older factories and modern industrial units in Bachmann's Scenecraft range, such as a two-storey office block that will combine with the modern unit. Bachmann also produces oil tanks and a modern industrial chimney. Another manufacturer worth looking at is Ten Commandments who again produce both older and modern factory units, although these samples are all produced in low relief.

WAREHOUSES AND STORAGE UNITS

After the Industrial Revolution there was a great need to move raw materials and goods around the country. There was also increased demand for imported raw materials. These goods and materials would need covered storage and this gave rise to the building of multi-storeyed warehouses. Originally warehouses were built along the quaysides at ports. As canals and, later, the railways spread across the country, warehousing became a common sight in

A double-gabled warehouse belonging to Fellows Morton & Clayton, who were major goods shippers on the canal system. This building, now restored, is at the Castle Lock Basin in Nottingham.

every urban centre. Warehouses were often built over a canal or had railway tracks running inside the building, so enabling goods to be loaded or unloaded under cover. Most warehouses had a series of landings with doors on each floor. These were positioned

This arrangement is also seen on a warehouse at Halifax, West Yorkshire.

This multi-floor warehouse in Gloucester docks is typical of buildings found at ports and the larger railway goods depots. Note that the gable end of the building faces the quayside with loading doors fitted to each floor. The weathering to the woodwork of the doors is a feature worth trying to recreate on a model.

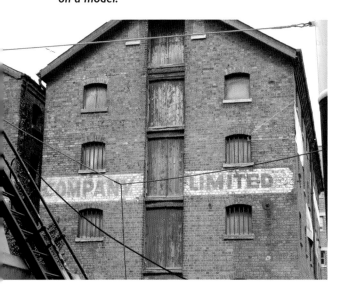

Along the side of the warehouse there is a series of doors, with a gable over the top door. A small pulley system has been fixed to this, so that goods could be pulled up to each floor, and there is a loading dock to the ground-floor doors. Note the weathering to Yorkshire gritstone from which this building is constructed.

The loading doors of the warehouses and mills often included a lucam or hoist house, which offered some protection while loading or unloading. Most, like this example on my model of 'Taw Valley Mills', were built from timber. For the model I used styrene strip to make a frame and 'Evergreen' pre-grooved styrene sheet over the top to create the boarded cladding. The barge-boards combined with the finial came from a spare set intended for the Ratio signal box kit and the support brackets were taken from another kit.

one above the other, either in the centre or at the gable end. This type of building would have a swing-out post crane or top beam-mounted crane installed to haul the goods up to each floor. A cover for the external loading and unloading system was provided, either with an extended roof or canopy, or with a wooden boxed-in structure fixed to the top floor or floors. This construction, known as a lucam or hoist house, was a common feature on both mills and warehouses. Larger warehouses, especially those in the docks and railway trans-shipment depots, had internal lifts to move goods from floor to floor. These were often powered by hydraulics and would have a power house combined to operate this system. Railway yards and canal wharfs would have loading and trans-shipment docks, usually provided with a covered roof or canopy, although the sides would be left open.

Storage is still required today, although the buildings have changed to meet modern needs. Large prefabricated boxes, which have become the standard building type for this purpose, are to be found on

This photograph shows the Grade 2 listed Grain Warehouse no. 2 next to Burton upon Trent station. The building has recently been converted into a Travelodge. The wooden hoist houses are evident on the side of the building, here occupying two floors and sets of doors.

industrial estates on the outskirts of urban areas and at distribution parks located alongside the network of major roads and motorways. Since the 1980s the preferred way of transporting the majority of goods around the country has been by road. Our ways of shopping have changed dramatically, too, and the high street is gradually becoming a thing of the past, with the increasing importance of retail centres on the edge of urban areas easily accessible by car, rather than in the centre. This trend has been reinforced by the introduction of internet shopping, where goods can be purchased without leaving home.

Ports have also changed with different methods of shipping the goods. The familiar cranes have all

An Aspinall 0-6-0 St shunts the vegetable warehouse on Martin Nield's pre-grouping layout 'Eccleston'. The warehouse was built by Andy Thompson, and is based on photographs of a warehouse in Bursclough, Lancashire.

Much more simple lines and construction are used today. Most modern warehouses and storage units have low brick plinth walls supporting a steel prefabricated frame clad with metal siding sheeting. They are not as pleasing aesthetically as their Victorian counterparts, but this design will be your prototype if you are modelling a modern image.

gone, as well as the large warehouse complexes (although some of these have been converted into luxury apartments). Goods are now imported and exported on giant container ships, which are handled at massive semi-automated container ports, such as Felixstowe.

Another change has seen the increasing use of air transport for freight. The facility to move smaller consignments by this method has seen the need for constructing large storage units at all of the major airports. Organizations such as the Royal Mail and DHL now transport mail and parcels for long distances by air rather than by rail.

MAKING MODELS OF WAREHOUSES

Models of earlier types of warehouse can be made from the same materials and methods as described above for mills and factories, so I will

This wide view looking across the platforms to the large LMS Railway grain warehouse in the background shows how much model can be fitted into a small space. This is because the warehouse has been modelled in low relief, and creates its own backdrop to this part of the layout. Photo: John Hancock

A double-gabled canal warehouse, with twin loading doors to the left-hand gable. This model was constructed in low relief, using foam board for the shell, with a skin of Das modelling clay applied before scribing the stonework. All the painting and weathering was created using artists' oil paints.

concentrate here on the added details needed for these buildings. One feature that is common to the warehouse is the presence of loading doors and landings on each floor, often with a lucam. These can be constructed easily from pre-scribed vertical or horizontal boarding, available in styrene sheet from Slater's or Evergreen, attached to a frame of styrene strip. Alternatively you can use card and scribe the boarding yourself. If the lucam and loading doors appear on the gable end of the building, the roof will need to extend over the lucam as well. The lucam is usually supported on a pair of cast metal

brackets, which can be modelled using the many etched brass samples on the market. Look at Scale Link or Langley Models for 4mm scale brackets and S&D Models for 7mm scale, although these will be produced as white metal castings rather than brass etchings. Plastic and laser cut versions may also be available from various suppliers. All the doors can be fabricated from pre-scribed styrene sheet or from card in the same way as the panelling to the lucam. Hinges can be added from thin styrene strip or you can use etched brass ones that are now available. Another detail that appears on ground-floor

A model warehouse under construction for a 4mm master to add to the Skytrex range. The shell was made from a high density cardboard before covering in a skin of Das modelling clay. Once dry the surface was scribed out to replicate the irregular stone used on this building.

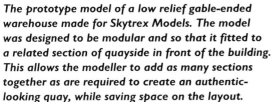

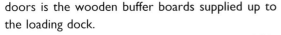

The prototype model of a low relief gable-ended warehouse made for Skytrex Models. The model was designed to be modular and so that it fitted to a related section of quayside in front of the building. This allows the modeller to add as many sections together as are required to create an authentic-looking quay, while saving space on the layout.

The finished painted and weathered Skytrex warehouse kit in low relief. Oil paints were again used to paint the resin model: a grey primer was applied first to allow the paint to key, then a build-up of dry brushing gave a seemingly authentic finish.

doors is the wooden buffer boards supplied up to the loading dock.

There are numerous kits of warehouses available in both card and resin. Metcalfe and Bilt-eezi produce printed card versions, while Skytrex has a range of warehouses in low relief in both 7mm and 4mm scales, including two versions of a stone-built gable

Close-up of the bottom doors with the loading dock below. Note the wooden buffer provided for carts and wagons to run up to.

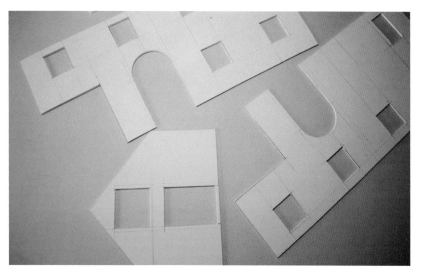

The cut-out components laid out ready for assembly. This was a commissioned model of a warehouse to accompany a water mill.

The front and end elevations of the warehouse now assembled to make the basic shell of the building. The 6mm and 3mm foam board, and the mounting board, are readily available from crafts suppliers.

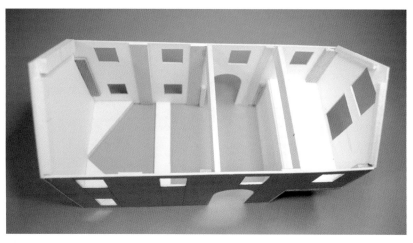

An overhead view of the shell, illustrating the amount of bracing needed by a large building such as a warehouse. As much bracing as possible should be used to prevent the model from warping when the building's skin is added. In this case Das modelling clay was applied to replicate the stone.

The finished model of the warehouse. A slate roof was added to the building and a wooden-boarded hoist house to the front gable end was constructed from card, with the boarded cladding made from hand-scored thin card. The whole model was painted using artists' oil paints (see Chapter 5).

end warehouse in the 7mm range, with open and boxed-in lucam. I have included the finished results from building and painting one of these simple and effective kits.

Good results can be obtained when modelling the modern warehouse or storage unit by using styrene sheet on a frame of styrene strip. The corrugated metal cladding can also be fabricated from styrene siding sheet from Evergreen. The modern storage unit has been covered in the resin kit market: Ten Commandments, for example, produces warehousing for the modern image railway modeller, including some low relief samples. Off-the-shelf models are available from the Bachmann Scenecraft range

COLLIERIES, FOUNDRIES, POTTERIES AND THE GASWORKS

Deposits of coal measures can be found in many parts of Britain at various depths, depending on the geology and how they were laid down. Coal mining developed into a vital industry supplying fossil fuel to serve just about every other industry, form of transport, services and domestic homes. Mining started with small pits and adits to reach coal measures close to the surface. To reach the deeper seams, shafts would need to be sunk. The distinctive pithead gear soon became a common sight in the landscape. The early and smaller collieries had simple headstocks constructed from timber, alongside which there would be the winding house with a stationary steam-powered engine inside. This would operate the cages to transport the miners and the loaded tubs of coal up and down the shaft. The engine would require a boiler, housed either in a separate building or within the engine house, a chimney and some provision for storing fuel for the boilers. Buildings known as screens were needed to wash and then grade the coal. A lamp room, stables for the pit ponies and other buildings would also be clustered around the shaft. Later coal mines would see impressive structures constructed from steel, while brick or even concrete might be used for the pit headgear. The larger collieries would have more associated buildings, including the pithead baths, maintenance sheds and stores. The more modern collieries would also have extensive conveyor systems to carry the graded coal to loading areas.

Another feature of the colliery would be the waste tip. Early tips had a distinctive conical shape and it appears they often had a reddish colour caused by instant combustion turning the black coal waste to red ash. Later methods of tipping would see them constantly being flattened by earth-moving vehicles. One way of moving the waste material away from the pithead to the tip was in loaded tubs carried by an aerial ropeway system. Some of the collieries on the North East coast used this system to tip their waste out to sea: the closing scenes of *Get Carter* (1971), filmed at Horden Beach, County Durham, come to mind.

MODELLING COLLIERIES

If you are building a model layout based on an industrial area, a small colliery would provide an interesting feature with plenty of potential for including some private or general sidings serving the colliery. If you are clever with the design it need not take up too much room, perhaps fitted into a corner of the layout. Creating some of the buildings in low relief would save even more space but still give you a good representation (for more detail on low relief, see Chapter 4).

The early style of headstocks can be fabricated from balsa or deal strip wood. You could also use

The head stocks of a small colliery. In a rebuilt form it is part of Blists Hill Victorian Town at Ironbridge.

styrene strip for the framework, but wood gives a more authentic result. For the wheel, you might be able to find something appropriate in white metal: I always look through the bit trays on the Langley Models stand at exhibitions. If you are modelling in 7mm scale, one of the cartwheels supplied by Duncan Models could probably be adapted for this purpose.

The buildings can be built from a variety of materials, although you won't go far wrong if you stick with those already described above for other industrial buildings. You will most likely need to construct a chimney to go with the boiler house. As well as the methods described above, however, if you are looking for a round-barrelled chimney it might be easier to use a kit from the likes of Skytrex.

There are a few kits on the market and even some off-the-shelf models. Bachmann's Scenecraft range, for example, has a number of colliery

A wide view of the colliery showing the timber-built head stocks and brick-built winding house. The black building, clad in corrugated iron sheet, is the boiler house, complete with metal chimney. This would make an interesting model for many model railway layouts depicting an urban scene.

buildings marketed under the collective fictitious name of 'Hampton Heath Colliery'. These include the headstocks, winding house, fan house, explosives magazine store, pit blacksmith's, sawmill, pithead baths and pitprop stacks.

IRON FOUNDRIES AND ROLLING MILLS

While the smelting of metal ores in Britain goes back more than four millennia, it was the Industrial Revolution that would see this industry expand greatly with the start of mass production. Until this time, the village blacksmith would have been responsible for creating all the items that needed to be fabricated from iron. Originally coal was the main fuel burned to bring the furnace up to temperature, but the carbon produced would create problems with the casting methods used. Pre-burning the carbon off in an oven produced coke, which burns pure and at the much higher temperatures required

The iron foundry at Blists Hill Victorian Town, showing the water tanks used to cool off the castings.

The main casting shop of G. R. Morton's Ironworks at Blists Hill.

This impressive industrial building is the blast furnace. The tall structure is the coke oven. Coke was burned to give a purer quality iron.

to smelt the ore and create good quality iron. The coke ovens became a major part of the iron foundry and this heavy industry became established all over the country.

POTTERIES AND BRICKWORKS

Stoke on Trent was the best-known area of the country for the production of ceramics: indeed, the towns neighbouring Stoke became known collectively as 'The Potteries'. Many other locations had small potteries and the familiar bottle ovens became a common sight. South Derbyshire, for example, boasted many potteries producing fine ceramics as well as domestic sanitary ware. Ceramic works in the area are still making pipes and chimney pots, including a number of small ceramic businesses

These magnificent examples of the distinctive bottle ovens are at the Gladstone Pottery Museum in Longton. Until the 1960s the skyline of the pottery towns surrounding Stoke-on-Trent contained hundreds of bottle ovens, all belching smoke and choking the atmosphere. The Clean Air Acts of the late 1950s would see the demise of the structures as the potteries were forced to turn to gas-fired kilns. Other ceramic wares fired in kilns included pipes, roof ware and bricks.

The bottle ovens would be surrounded by other buildings associated with the pottery industry. The pottery workshop or pot bank shown here provided the prototype for a commissioned model.

established to produce chimney pots, roof ware and tiles to meet the demand for restoration projects.

Many urban buildings were finished with ceramic embellishments, either along the ridge of the roof or decorating the facades. This type of architectural detail, especially on the roof, was not easily accessible to the general public, and yet it was common during the Victorian period. The history of ceramic roofware goes back to the Greeks and the Romans, who used terracotta tiles for decoration as well as function. Next time you walk down the high street, just take a little time to look up at some of the buildings. The market is limited, however, when it comes to finding miniature versions of this type of decoration to use on models, especially in the smaller scales, although S&D Models supply a few for 7mm scale buildings. Otherwise it is a case of sculpting them from materials such as Milliput epoxy putty. If you need a number of the same design, it might be worth considering sculpting a master, making a mould and casting reproductions in resin.

Modelling Potteries and Brickworks

The first image that springs to mind when considering the potteries and associated workshops that produce ceramic ware, from crockery to pipes and bricks, would be that of the bottle-shaped ovens used to bake the clay. This structure became synonymous with this industry. During the late nineteenth century and the early twentieth century there were hundreds of bottle ovens belching out smoke across the skyline of the Stoke area of Staffordshire. The ovens differed slightly in shape depending on the firing method used. The outer part of the structure, the bottle shape, was known as the hovel. This acted as a chimney, taking away the smoke, and created the draught as well as protecting the oven inside. The inner part of the oven proper is a round structure with a domed roof. In most cases, however, this would not be visible on a model, so we need to concentrate only on the bottle oven exterior.

To create this shape is not easy. The best solution if you are modelling one from scratch is to turn it from wood on a lathe. If you don't possess such equipment, you could commission a wood turner to make one for you. (You might perhaps meet one at a craft centre or craft fair.) You will need to supply a scale drawing, of course. I have made a few bottle ovens for private commissions. When I was asked to create the masters from which resin castings would be made for the Skytrex range, I persuaded a good friend who is a qualified pattern maker to turn originals from my drawings. Another alternative might be to use an actual bottle, if you can find one the right size, although you may have to cut this down or sink the bottom half into the baseboard as the model will need only the upper half with the neck. Once covered with a plaster skin this may look fairly convincing. Even if you use the turned wood idea, you will still need to coat this with a skin to give the surface texture required. Brush on a thin skin of

A bottle kiln, with attached workshop, produced in 7mm scale resin kit form by Skytrex Models. I was responsible for the master of this casting, with every brick scribed in from top to bottom.

plaster made by mixing No More Cracks plaster filler with PVA to the consistency of 60 per cent plaster to 40 per cent adhesive. Once dry, this can be scribed with all the brickwork. This can be a daunting task, so if the bottle oven is situated at the back of your layout you might get away with a paint effect on the plaster that gives a convincing result without going to all that trouble. All bottle ovens feature expansion bands (bonts) around the structure, which are necessary due to the extreme forces of expansion and contraction brought about when firing. These can be made from a strip of card or styrene, with some bolt joiners fabricated from styrene rod or wire. A door will also have to be provided to give access to the kiln inside. This can be made up from card and

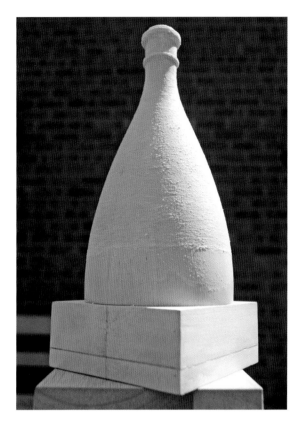

The bottle oven in its early stages. In order to create the distinctive shape, I commissioned a friend to turn this in his lathe to my drawings. The first coat of plaster filler has been applied to create the brick skin.

the gap filled with clay or Milliput. The planked door itself can be made from scribing card or from pre-scribed styrene sheet material. Any door furniture can be made in the usual way described earlier. The associated buildings, such as workshops and stores, are made in the same way and using the same materials as those used earlier for other industrial buildings, with similar windows and other fittings.

Kits and Off-the-Shelf Models of Bottle Ovens

Although a card kit with workshop was formerly available in 4mm scale from Novus W&T, this type of structure has been rare to find. Skytrex, however,

The completed model of the pottery workshop with the integral bottle oven protruding through the roof.

The chimney on the model bottle oven. Note the iron expansion bands or 'bonts', the flashing where the oven meets the roof, the build-up of soot around the chimney and the rain staining to the roof.

has recently introduced a bottle oven available in both 7mm and 4mm scale. I can vouch for the detail on the resin castings since I scribed in every brick on both the masters. They also supply the door in position and the expansion bands. All that is required is painting and weathering. The 7mm model also has the option of combining it with a pottery workshop and the kiln. Both a version built from scratch and the resin castings can be painted using artists' oil paints, although the latter will first need to be primed with undercoat. I would recommend grey acrylic primer spray paint to achieve the best base. Use a coat of thinned-down oil paint with a mix of Titanium White and just a touch of Naples Yellow to achieve the mortar colour. Mixes of Warm Red, Indian Red, Chrome Orange and Naples Yellow will create the brick colour when dry brushed on. The expansion bands should be picked out in a dark grey with a rust brown dry brushed over the top. The door should be painted light grey or brown. The finished structure will need extensive weathering by dry brushing on a dark grey colour mixed from Payne's Grey and Lamp Black. In particular you should recreate the effect of the build-up of soot around the chimney. If you possess an air brush you could use this, but careful dry brushing should give the desired effect. Always look at photographs of the prototype to see just how this appears. To finish off some streaking

The workshop's roof under construction. The slates have been cut from card and applied in strips overlapping each other up to the roof's apex.

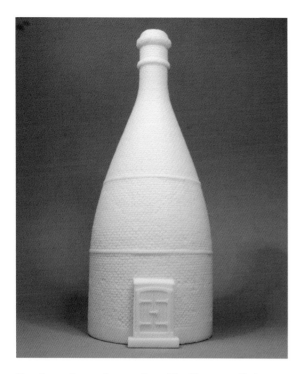

For the resin casting produced by Skytrex, all the brick coursing was scribed into a plaster skin. The basic shape was again turned on the lathe.

The first coat of red primer is added to the resin casting to give the base colour to the brickwork.

A wash of oil paint is added to create the mortar and then wiped away with a paper towel, leaving it just in the mortar gaps.

The finished painted model: all the brickwork and weathering has been created by dry brushing.

can be added running down from the bands. Also try and add some white powder: the residue left from scribing out can be used for this. When all the other paint has completely dried off, rub some of the white powder residue from scribing out into areas to give the effect of re-mortared brick masonry and seal it into position with a light coat of matt artists' fixative spray. This treatment can look very authentic provided it is not overdone.

MODELLING BRICKWORKS AND PIPEWORKS

Kilns for firing bricks and clay pipes could be seen in many parts of the country, so they would not look out of place on most urban layouts. The construction of brick kilns was similar to that of bottle ovens, although the structure would be much squatter with a round base and sloping walls, topped with a dome.

A scratch-built kiln could again be turned from wood or perhaps could be built from an ice cream tub. As with the bottle oven, a skin of plaster filler or Das modelling clay needs to be added and then once again it is down to scribing out all the brickwork. The dome may be created by building it up from clay and sculpting it into the shape of a dome. This may need a little cleaning up with sandpaper before it too is scribed to make the brickwork that forms the domed top. The brickworks will require a chimney connected to the flues from the kilns. The prototypes would often have a stack with a square profile, which can easily be constructed using card or styrene sheet with the square sides then covered with embossed brick styrene sheet. Try to ensure that the coursing is level on all four sides. Instead of the expansion bands found on a round chimney or kiln, the square construction requires tie bars fitted at a regular spacing from the bottom to the top of the stack. To model these, corner braces should first be added to all four sides of the stack using styrene angle strip in a size appropriate for the scale of your model. Once all the corner braces are complete, the tie bars can then be added using styrene rod, again of an appropriate diameter. Glue the bars to the corner-braced angle iron and trim off any excess,

The typical square profile chimney used as the flue for most brick and pipe works. Note the corner braces and the tie bars fitted.

making sure that the bars are level on all four sides and are equally spaced up the stack. The chimney should then be painted as described for the bottle ovens.

GASWORKS

Until the 1960s, when the process began of converting every home in the country to be able to use gas from the North Sea, coal gas was processed at the local gasworks to supply all the services and domestic supply. A gasworks would make an interesting feature for a corner of any model railway: it would usually be built close to or alongside the railway line and have private sidings to bring in the coal by rail.

This 'North Lights' factory building at the rear of Eccleston is in mock-up form. It is always worth building a mock-up of a large building first to see how it will fit and relate to other buildings around it.

Modelling a Gasworks

A gasworks complex consisted of a number of buildings to process the gas and then a means of storing it. The buildings were single-storey structures with typical industrial features, built from brick with multi-paned, arched metal windows. The roofs were either gabled or hipped in style and covered in Welsh slates. The processing buildings were fitted with ventilators. A major feature of the works would be the chimney, together with its accompanying piping and valves. You might be able to convert an off-the-shelf model or 'kit bash' some of the engine shed kits that are readily available: plastic examples such as those by Dapol (once part of the Airfix range) and Ratio Models come to mind, and I am sure something will be available in card. The yards of pipes required can be constructed from those supplied by Knightwing. A gas holder can be fabricated

from two cut-down uPVC pipes. One should be of slightly smaller diameter so that it slides inside the larger one. The next job is to replicate the curved steel plates from which the prototype tank would be constructed. One method would be to cut individual plates from adhesive-backed paper, although they will first have to be marked out to size. Rivets can be added to the plates using a small ball-tipped embossing tool, lightly punching in the rivets from the back of the paper before carefully cutting it into the separate plates. You can then start assembling the plates on the round sides of the pipes in the same way as stretcher bonding used in brickwork. The top or cap that needs to be added to the smaller diameter top tank usually had a slight dome, which is not easy to replicate on a model. One suggestion would be to create it using the bottom of a plastic ice cream or margarine tub, or something similar. A frame will have to be constructed to allow the two tanks to move up and down. The tanks would rise when filled with gas and fall as they emptied, with the lower tank sinking into a well in the ground. To allow the tanks to move up and down, wheels are attached to the sides, which run freely on rails fitted to the inside of the framework. There are plenty of small wheels on the market that would be of an appropriate size. If your model is in 4mm scale, use wheels intended for 2mm rolling stock; for a 7mm model use wheels intended for 4mm stock. The wheels will be carried in frames or brackets, looking like upside-down casters. The framework can be made from Plastruct or Evergreen truss girders. This consists of a number of verticals with the rails added, and stretcher trusses holding the frame together laterally. Diagonal strengthening bars that connect the main verticals can be modelled using styrene rod or strip. Sometimes the vertical frame had decorative tops like finials. Once the construction is complete, all that remains is to paint it

and weather it. Spray paints give a neat finish, while the weathering, including rust, can be dry brushed on afterwards.

If you find building a gas holder from scratch a daunting task, there is a ready-made version available from the Hornby Skaledale range in 4mm scale. Other related buildings in this range, under the name of 'Skaledale Gasworks', include a retort house with a square chimney, a workshop or stores, purifiers and condenser units. Others may be found on the market as off-the-shelf examples or as kits.

BREWERIES AND MALT-HOUSES

The art of brewing good ale is down to special minerals found in watercourses. In the Midlands the centre of the brewing industry became Burton upon Trent, owing to the deposits of gypsum in the area's water. The Benedictine monks of Burton Abbey

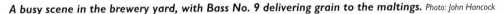

A busy scene in the brewery yard, with Bass No. 9 delivering grain to the maltings. Photo: John Hancock

saw the potential of the waters and started what eventually became a major industry that proudly proclaimed Burton as the 'Brewing Capital of the World'. Burton was not alone, of course, and many towns had breweries associated with them. The breweries and the Scottish whisky distilleries relied heavily on the railways to bring in the raw materials and distribute the finished product. The larger establishments had private sidings or even lines running right into the brewery buildings. The private railways of Burton upon Trent were a prominent feature of the town, with tracks crossing the main streets at numerous level crossings.

The principal building was the tower brewery, where the process of brewing was undertaken. The tall building was purpose built so that each floor from top to bottom accommodated a stage in the production. The water would be stored at the very top of the tower in a large tank. Each floor had windows and panels of louvred ventilators. The brewery's boiler house, with its chimney, would either be attached or in close proximity to the main building. The tall chimneys of the numerous breweries in Burton upon Trent made its skyline resemble that of the Lancashire mill towns. Other associated buildings included racking rooms and the long Union

The tower brewery building with the boiler house and chimney attached.

Part of the extensive brewery buildings belonging to Samuel Allsopp and Sons (later merged with Ind Coope) at Burton. Note the water tank on top of the building to the right.

A model of a Midland Railway tank house. The construction of the tank is very similar to that used on the brewery buildings.

The main brewery buildings of the Bass New Brewery in Burton upon Trent.

The tower brewery of Marston's Albion complex stands on the western edge of Burton. The water tank is clearly visible at the top of the tower, with the sides of the tank used to promote the company name. It was a common practice to position the tank at the top, allowing the water to be gravity fed for use in the brewing processes on each floor.

The four floors of Everards Trent Brewery, Burton. The brewhouse is completely square with four arched reveals containing the windows and louvre vents. The roof is a four-sided pyramid with a central projecting roof vent that has its own pyramidal roof. Although the building has been turned into luxury apartments, it retains most of its original features.

rooms, required for a method of finishing the beer that was unique to Burton.

Alongside the breweries there were malt-houses, known as maltings, where the barley and other grains would be processed. The top floor of these multi-storey buildings would be reserved for storing the grain. This would require the addition of landings and hoist houses by which sacks of grain would be hauled up from wagons. The barley was first steeped with water, causing the grain to start germinating. This would then be spread out over the vast, low floors and turned manually – a back-breaking job – at regular intervals by maltsters. Heat was introduced and the malt was kiln dried before being taken to the brewery as a major ingredient in the production of beer. Malt-houses with built-in kilns came in different styles. The kilns had steep pitched roofs with some kind of ventilation positioned at the top. The most

This view of the large gable end of the Crown Maltings in Burton upon Trent clearly shows the blind arches, an architectural feature seen in most of the town's brewery buildings.

A mix of terraced housing and industrial buildings. Pre-printed card buildings can have a place at the back of the layout, where relief detail is not too obvious. Photo: Andy Peters

A malt-house in Derby with the drying kiln positioned at one end of the building.

Multi-storey factory buildings and a boiler house on a layout still under construction by the Gresley Model Railway Group. Photo: Andy Peters

This large malt-house was part of the Clarence Street Maltings, belonging to the Peter Walker Brewery. The kiln has a steep hipped roof fitted with a top louvre vent. The hoist house, supported on a pair of large brackets, was positioned to haul grain up to the top floors of the drying kiln.

The roof line of the drying kilns at the former Salts Walsitch Maltings. This building featured a double steep hipped roof to accommodate three tall vents to each roof. The vents were tapered and had large pyramid-shaped caps. The roof covering was Welsh slate with lead flashings to the corners.

This wider view of the maltings shows the double row of kilns in the centre, flanked on both sides by the malt-house. The building has been converted for commercial use, but it retains many of its original features, apart from the large roller shutter doors. Note the buttressed brick columns and the filled-in window reveals.

common style used long louvred vents running the length of the roofs. Some had individual louvre vents with pyramid caps. Another style was for the kiln house to have square or octagonal walls and a tall pyramidal or conical roof crowned by a cowl vent. A wind vane was fitted to direct the cowl into the desired direction. This type of kiln house was not unlike the familiar oast houses of Kent, where hops were kiln dried before being shipped to the breweries. Smaller buildings found in the brewery yard included the cooperage, cask washing plant, stables and the weighbridge offices. There would also be the ale docks, where the full casks were stored ready for loading on to wagons.

ABOVE, LEFT: *Another form of hoist house was the open balcony platform type, which was open on the sides but retained a gable roof. It was supported on brackets to give some protection when hauling up sacks of grain. This sample can still be seen on the Plough Maltings, Horninglow Street, oppposite Burton's National Brewery Centre.*

ABOVE, RIGHT: *This is the modern way of providing malt for the brewing process. Large aluminium silos have replaced the traditional malt-houses with an automated processing plant. Shining in the late summer sun, these form part of the former Bass brewery now owned by the US company Coors.*

LEFT: *The old and the new. The modern steel chimney installed for the boiler rooms at the Coors Brewery contrasts dramatically with the old racking rooms that used to belong to the Bass New Brewery. These building have now been converted into the Brewhouse Arts Centre.*

Bass No.9 delivering grain; note the construction of the malt houses with wooden hoist houses to lift the grain to the upper floors. Photo: John Hancock

MODELLING BREWERIES AND MALTINGS

Although the complex might be fairly large, a brewery would make an excellent addition to any urban model railway layout. The railway played an important part in the brewing process, bringing in the raw materials and transporting out the finished ale. In larger breweries the tracks would run around and sometimes into the buildings. This gives the modeller plenty of opportunities to create a busy and convincing industrial scene.

The tower brewery can be constructed from a card shell with plenty of bracing to strengthen the corners as the building will require many windows and vent apertures to be cut out. The tower will be at least four storeys high with a water tank accommodated on top. Most breweries have thick masonry made from brick or local stone. The shell will therefore need a covering of embossed brick or stone styrene sheet, with the corner joins treated as

described earlier. Alternatively you could scribe the stone into a skin of Das modelling clay. Although this method will take longer, it will achieve better results if the stone is large or irregular. As with any building it is advisable to add the windows, vents and doors before the roof is added. For the most part brewery buildings would be fitted with multi-paned metal frames, usually with a curved top. Centre-pivoted lights would also be essential for extra ventilation. Wooden frames were not practical in the environment of the brewing process since the water vapour created would cause the frame to rot. Louvre vents, however, were made from timber. I would recommend using etched or laser-cut brass frames for both the windows and vents (the latter may be had from GT Models or Scale Link). Louvres can also be made by overlapping styrene or card strip.

Once the windows, vent panels and doors have been fitted, the roof can then be fixed into position. This would feature a hipped roof with an additional

A bird's-eye view looking down onto the brewery yard and the ale dock. This makes a very interesting industrial scene to this corner of the 'Wychnor' layout. Photo: John Hancock

hipped or gable-roofed top vent with extra windows inserted. The roof space also accommodated the large tank from which the water supply was fed by gravity for use in all the brewing processes situated below. The model's roof can be made from card, starting with a flat base. Trusses are then added, again made from card or foam board, to support the panels that make up the roof. Some towers, such as the Everards Trent (or Tiger) Brewery in Burton upon Trent, were built totally square and featured a pyramid roof. The top vent would also be crowned with a pyramid roof and occasionally a flagpole or decorative finial. The roof covering would generally be of Welsh slates, although tiles were preferred in some areas. The sides of the top vent can be made in the same way as the vent panels. The slates or tiles are made by cutting

thin card in the usual way. The edges and any joins would have received lead flashings, which can be made from thin paper or foil. If the prototype's water tank is located here it will have to be assembled into the roof and supported on the flat base. The tank can be fabricated from card or styrene sheet, with Plastruct or Evergreen right-angled strip added around the top. If you wish to go further with the detail and include individual panels to the tank, brass etchings are available that might provide just what you are looking for. Details like the guttering and downpipes can be added to finish the construction.

Most tower breweries had a hoist house to haul grain and hops up to the top floors. These were made from wooden frames clad with timber planking and sometimes incorporated a window and elaborate

One of the brewery's boiler houses. Note the open-sided prefabricated building that has been provided with corrugated cladding, supplied just to give enough shelter. Also of interest is the 'Hawthorn Leslie' saddle tank belonging to 'Marston Thompson & Evershed Brewery'. Photo: John Hancock

barge-boards terminating with a finial. This extension can be constructed from a styrene strip frame faced with pre-scribed planking, also in styrene, or alternatively you could scribe card to make the planking. Barge-boards may have to be etched or laser cut depending on how elaborate they are. A pair of cast iron brackets would also be required to support the structure as it cantilevered out from the main wall. Etched or laser-cut ones are available from Scale Link and Langley Models, or you could try the brackets supplied for signals, such as those offered in 4mm or 7mm scale from Wizard Models.

Cast iron tie-bar plates were a feature of many brewery buildings.

The octagonal kiln of the Goat Maltings, belonging to the Peter Walker Brewery, was unique in Burton, with a single conical roof following the octagonal shape. A cowl vent was provided to the top with an unusual copper wind vane shaped like a goat.

Alongside or built onto the side of the tower brewery would be the boiler house, complete with a tall chimney. A water tower would also be needed if a tank was not accommodated within the roof of the brewery. The boiler house would be constructed from the same materials as the main building and have windows to match. Large doors were often provided to load coal into the boilers. The roof profile could be either hipped or have a shallow-pitched gable, usually with a louvred vent on top or individual roof ventilators situated along the roof pitch or ridge. The model is made in the same way as that of the main building, using pre-scribed styrene planking for the doors. The individual ventilators can be added using resin mushroom vents from Skytrex. The external pipework fitted to provide hot water

The south malt-house kiln in the Clarence Street complex features a tall hipped roof with both types of vent provided. The goat-shaped wind vane can be seen on the conical roof in the background.

or steam to other parts of the brewery can be fabricated from kits by Knightwing or Ratio Models.

The boiler house will not be complete without a chimney, which can either be constructed as described for mills and factories or you can use a ready-made one from Skytrex. The majority of brewery chimneys were of the round type, although octagonal profiles were also common; both types were seated on a square flue base.

The construction methods and materials when constructing a model malt-house are the same as have been described for modelling a textile mill. As with a mill, the building consisted of a series of floors, although the individual storeys were not as high and fewer windows were needed along each floor. The

A model of an ale dock canopy with the counting office set underneath. Windows were provided on all sides of the building so that every stage of loading could be observed.

The construction of a pyramid vent, a design commonly used to crown the steep roofs of the drying kilns.

UNDERNEATH THE ARCHES

This box shows how to paint and finish a lock-up business, found underneath the railway arches. Many small businesses occupied the space created by these arches in our towns and cities. The arches are supplied in 7mm scale in one piece of resin from Skytrex Models.

The unpainted resin panel. It consists of three brick railway arches with lock-up small businesses housed within.

The mortar colour was added first; it was mixed and applied using a thin wash of oil paint. Refer to Chapter 5 for the colours and mixing amounts used to achieve this.

This picture shows the mixing of oil paint, using an old ice cream tub lid as a palette. The colours used to achieve an authentic brick effect are listed in Chapter 5, though you should always refer to your prototype and replicate the colour as close as you can.

The final painting of the arches, with the brick colour added by dry brushing. The weathering has been added to the brickwork, and the lock-up door and window painted and weathered.

malt-houses would also include the kilns, needed to provide the constant heat required for the process of producing malt from grain.

The walls of the kiln were generally the same as those of the main malt-house, although the kiln at the Clarence Stret maltings of the Peter Walker Brewery in Burton was octagonal. Even on this structure, however, the detailing was the same as on the malt-house, apart from its shape. The main difference was the roof, which had very steep pitches to allow the heat to rise in the roof space and then be expelled through ventilators at the top; on the model these can be made from card. For the roof a flat base is assembled on top of the walls. Strips of balsa wood or foam board are added to the inside edge of the roof panel to support the panel running up to it. Once this has been glued together, a strip of masking tape is run down the join to make it extra strong. Most kilns had this extra steep hipped roof, although, some had a series of individual pyramid roofs or, in a few cases, an octagonal, conical roof. The roof covering was again generally thin slates,

Typical brewery buildings now converted into commercial offices.

The gatehouse to the Bass Middle Brewery. Note the ornate gritstone gate pillar. The entrance was always made to look as impressive as possible in order to emphasize to visitors the brewery's importance.

The tall original brew house of the old Allsopp's brewery. No expense was spared to give an ornate decorative finish to important Victorian industrial buildings. Modern industrial buildings, however, are built to be practical and lack the character of their predecessors.

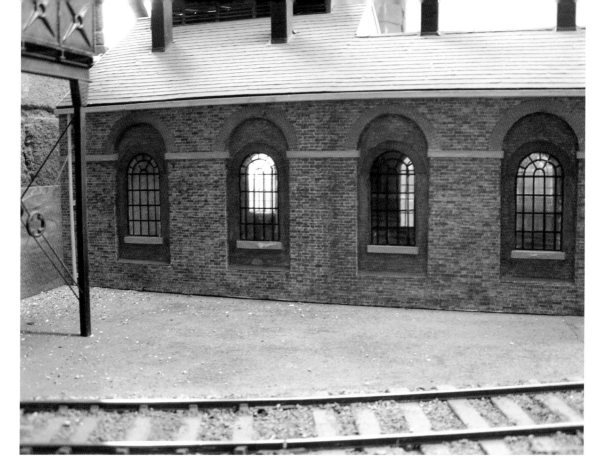

The private locomotive sheds of the brewery have been modelled by members of the Wychnor Model Railway group. Photo: John Hancock

although a few were fitted with tiles like the oast houses in Kent.

The most common style of ventilator fitted to the top of the kiln roof was tapered to a square open-sided vent with an overhanging metal pyramid cap. This can be made from either styrene strip or sheet or card and balsa strip. Conical roofed kilns would have a steel cowl, fitted with a wind vane. The cowl can be fabricated by making a cone from thin card and cutting the top and bottom at an angle of about 20 degrees. The wind vane can be added using two strips of card and a short length of styrene rod, fixed with superglue. The vane itself, cut from thin card to the shape required, is then fixed to this.

This now covers the main buildings to be found in the brewery yard, but there are a few more that will make a brewery model complete.

Cooperage

Most breweries would include a cooperage, a facility for making up the casks. The job of the cooper was very skilled, although over the last five decades this skill has been lost with the arrival of steel and aluminium casks. Two coopers are left employed in Burton to maintain the wooden barrels used for Marston's Burton Union system. The building would consist of one or two storeys, built in the style of the other buildings, with similar metal-framed windows and opening lights for ventilation. Good ventilation was essential to cope with pollution from the firing process used to finish the inside of the wooden casks. As a result the roof would feature louvred vents, either full length or a series. The building would also incorporate the store for seasoned timber and metal bands. The finished casks would be taken out to the yard, from where they went to the racking room to be filled with beer. Not all beers were brewed to be served as draught from casks. There was also demand for bottle beers, which required a building for the bottling process with a room to store and crate the finished product.

The brewery yard with the ale dock in the foreground,. Note the interesting weathering to the brickwork on the wall; it is small details like this that make our models become more realistic. Photo: John Hancock

Cask Washing Plant

The larger breweries also had facilities for reusing the casks, which went through a process of having their insides steam cleaned. It was important that they were cleaned thoroughly. The complex to carry out this process would consist of one store for the unclean casks and another for the completed clean casks. Between them, in the centre, would be the cleaning plant with a boiler house to create the vast amount of steam required. The style of building would again replicate those seen in the rest of the brewery yard. The roof could be either gabled or hipped, again with provision for plenty of ventilation from louvred top roof vents or a series of individual mushroom-type vents. To model the cask washing

plant building and its chimney, I would suggest following the procedures as described for the brewery's main boiler house. It will require numerous casks or barrels to dress and finish the model.

Stables

Until the 1950s horses still played a major role in any industrial yard, carrying goods and materials internally from one part of the brewery to another. Brewery Shire horses were also used to deliver the beer to the local public houses and hotels. This spectacle can still be seen on certain days in Devizes, Wiltshire, as they deliver beer from the Wadsworth Brewery. The stable blocks required to house and look after

This overall view of the corner of the 'Wychnor' layout shows the brewery locomotive sheds and yard with the canal wharf in front. It also features the terraced houses on Canal Street. Photo: John Hancock

the horses would match the other buildings, again with louvred roof vents, the main difference being the addition of stable doors.

Ale Dock

The ale dock comprised a raised platform with a canopy supplied to keep the weather off. This was built from a steel framework clad with timber or corrugated iron awnings. Those with timber cladding could even be finished with decorative valancing, similar to that used on stations. The roof profiles were usually either gabled or barrel shaped. A checking office positioned under the canopy was normally just a timber prefabricated building with large windows to view the loading.

To model the canopy, the framework can be fabricated by using styrene girders supplied by Plastruct or Evergreen, to which is fixed cladding made from embossed planked styrene sheet or you could try scribing your own planking onto card sheet. The gable roofs will require a covering of slates or corrugated materials. Slates can be cut by hand from thin card or you can use styrene sheet. The corrugated materials are all readily available in styrene sheet in building packs from Slater's, Evergreen and Wills. The best solution for a barrel roof canopy would be to use the vacuum-formed corrugated one produced by Ratio Models. You might also be able to adopt the Ratio kit intended for the carriage shed. The counting office can be constructed from pre-scribed

A busy goods yard is depicted in this photograph of 'Wychnor-on Trent'. Photo: John Hancock

styrene sheet or card, perhaps using the sash frames from the Wills building pack materials series. A door with a window will complete this small office.

Gatehouse and Weighbridge Office

The brewery yard will probably include a gatehouse and a weighbridge office, both positioned at or near to the gateway to the brewery. The architectural style of even these small buildings will still reflect the larger ones, sometimes having more ornate embellishments intended to give a good impression to anyone entering the yard. The same materials and methods can be used to make models of these buildings.

KITS AND OFF-THE-SHELF MODELS OF BREWERIES

A number of kits and off-the-shelf models of breweries and associated buildings are available.

A good kit of a complete brewery has been produced by Metcalfe Models. Unfortunately it belongs to the pre-printed card series and the masonry is not rendered in relief, but it can look good when positioned at the rear of the layout. There does not appear to be a brewery as such available from a plastic kit, although a few railway and other industrial buildings can be either adapted or 'kit-bashed' to make a reasonable representation of some brewery buildings.

The 'Oak Hill Brewery' from Bachmann's Scenecraft range is a fully painted off-the-shelf model of a brewery, although as this model doubles as a warehouse it does not represent a tower type of brewery. A low relief brick-built bonded warehouse from the same range would not look out of place alongside the brewery. Bachmann and Ten Commandments also produce handy sets of barrels. A boiler house, again available from Bachmann, would fit in well if

Eccleston goods shed. Most stations in an urban area would have provision for handling goods.

you choose to model a modern brewery. If you are modelling in 7mm scale the Skytrex boiler house is worth looking at. A brewery octagonal chimney was produced in the 'Scenecraft' range. The model was out of production at the time of writing, but you might be able to find one on eBay or at a toy and collectors' fair. The round and octagonal chimneys available from Skytrex would both make excellent models for a brewery.

This concludes the look at industrial buildings and how we might make miniature versions of them. I have concentrated on describing how to make models of some of our older industrial buildings, although the modern scene has not been left out completely. My intention was to give some idea of what buildings can be added to make a realistic and convincing urban scene for your model railway.

CHAPTER TWO

DOMESTIC HOUSING

GEORGIAN AND REGENCY TOWN HOUSES

The Industrial Revolution brought much wealth to the owners of the new industries during the eighteenth and nineteenth centuries. Impressive town houses were erected for this class in the fast developing towns and cities, including the major ports and the fashionable seaside resorts.

Large terraces were built with multiple floors and half-basements that raised the ground floors so the house had to be accessed by steps, enhancing the effect. The finest houses had separate accommodation for the servants away from the family, sometimes in extensions or service rooms situated at the back of the properties with a mews being built in the rear yard. Other town houses were built as semi-detached or detached houses known as villas. These were generally built in the growing suburbs, rather than in the town or city centres. The exterior style incorporated the classical orders and forms of decoration that were then in vogue. Fine cut stone

was fashionable but expensive, so brick was used. A false finish to recreate the look of stone, however, could be achieved by adding a render called stucco, into which fine lines were traced to imitate regular stone coursing. The effect was enhanced by adding white, beige or grey paint. Some of the richer owners and merchants built mock castles in a fanciful style popularly known as 'Gothick'.

The windows favoured in Georgian houses were of the deep, multi-paned sash style. The Regency period would also see shallow bow and French windows, sometimes with balconies and window guards. Exterior ironwork became a feature, sometimes elaborate and intricate. Ornamental moulded window and door surrounds or lintels were also common.

Doors were both tall and wide, constructed with six panels or more. No expense was spared with door furniture, as this would be noticed by everyone entering the house. Above these large, impressive doors would be a distinctive fan-shaped window or ornamental hoods and tracery.

The rich mill owners lived in large Georgian town houses that lined the streets on the edge of the town centres.

Symonds House is a large town house constructed from stone ashlar masonry. All Georgian houses featured classical embellishments to the architecture.

After the Georgian period came the Regency, with town houses built in the style of large terraces. This example in North Street, Derby, illustrates the multiple storeys with basements.

The rooflines to these houses have a shallow-pitched hipped structure or a series of gables, which are often arranged across the width of the building instead of the length. These would have a central valley with a lead-lined gutter. Welsh slate would be the most common covering for both types, although tiles could also be found in certain parts of the country. A common practice, especially on the terraces, was to keep the roof pitch out of sight, contained behind a parapet. The facade up to the roofline would also feature a decorative cornice or elaborate stringcourse. Guttering and down-pipes would be square in profile, with the gutter shaped on the facing side if visible. Hoppers at the top of downpipes and at junctions were some-times decorated, although this would hardly be seen from ground level. Chimney stacks on the ridges were squat and wide as they contained a number of flues, with fireplaces being provided in every room. The stacks would be crowned with a row of chimney pots, the colours of which varied depending on the area.

A fashionable feature of the Regency period was the use of distinctive multiple-paned shallow bay windows. These on the first floor were often full height and included a balcony.

MODELLING GEORGIAN AND REGENCY TOWN HOUSES

The starting point, as with all models, has to be research, gathering information on a site visit to photograph the prototype. The next stage will require making scale drawings incorporating all your findings. If you are building a large terrace, I would recommend first putting together a mock-up. A multi-storey building of this size will have quite an impact on the layout, so as with the mill (*see* Chapter 1) it is a good idea to glue photocopies of your drawings onto the mock-up to see how it will fit into the scene and its effect on the surrounding buildings. It would also be worth going through this process will a semi-detached or detached villa. Another reason for the mock-up is that it will assist in making sure that everything in the finished model is in proportion in the three-dimensional plane. It

A pair of classical Georgian doors, dating from the second half of the eighteenth century, with a gable head and classical fanlight, which was designed to cast light into the long narrow hall and beyond. Earlier types tended to be rectangular, with a pattern made from wood or iron. Later examples had the characteristic semicircular shape with intricate patterns made from cast iron.

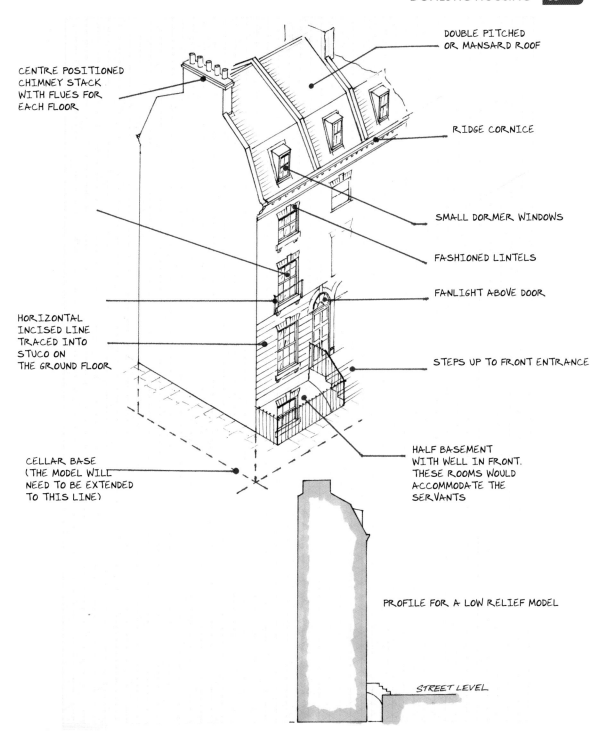

CENTRE POSITIONED CHIMNEY STACK WITH FLUES FOR EACH FLOOR

DOUBLE PITCHED OR MANSARD ROOF

RIDGE CORNICE

SMALL DORMER WINDOWS

FASHIONED LINTELS

FANLIGHT ABOVE DOOR

HORIZONTAL INCISED LINE TRACED INTO STUCO ON THE GROUND FLOOR

STEPS UP TO FRONT ENTRANCE

CELLAR BASE (THE MODEL WILL NEED TO BE EXTENDED TO THIS LINE)

HALF BASEMENT WITH WELL IN FRONT. THESE ROOMS WOULD ACCOMMODATE THE SERVANTS

PROFILE FOR A LOW RELIEF MODEL

STREET LEVEL

The construction of a Regency town terrace. Both the attic, with dormer windows taking advantage of the steep pitch to the roof, and the basement rooms would be reserved for the servants' quarters. The profile drawing shows how this building can be modelled in low relief to save space. The roof has been extended just over the apex and the chimney stack has been modelled in full. This will give the impression that the whole of the building is modelled.

A Regency town terrace with a shallow pitched roof. Note the extension to the front-facing wall with a parapet and the prominent cornice covering the join between the wall and roof. The deep sash windows on the first floor are fitted with shallow balconies.

will be important to ensure that the half-basements are visible on the model. This can be done by sinking the building into the baseboard or you can first build up a sub-base with the road and land level above the surface of the baseboard. This will require substantial planning, especially if the land is on a gradient and the terrace has to be stepped. In cases like this, first build a cardboard mock-up of the whole street or area in close proximity to the buildings. This sounds like a lot of work, but it is well worth making sure the foundations are correct in order to achieve a realistic model.

We can now look at constructing the model, starting with the carcass of the building, for which you should use artist mounting board. Transfer the drawing to this material, making sure you include all the windows in the half-basement. The next stage is to cut out all the windows and doors. If the prototype has no rendering, the card should be faced with embossed brick styrene sheet, selecting the correct bonding for this. Overlap the styrene on the corners and then trim off the surplus, creating a butt joint. It is likely that corner quoins will be needed. The easiest way to create them is by using the Wills ready-made corner quoins, although for a tall building you may have to splice together two strips or more. If the building has been rendered to give a stucco finish, this can be created on the surface of the mount board. In 4mm scale the plain surface will be good enough and, if you need to recreate the chasing, this can be lightly scored in with a scalpel or hobby knife. Use the same technique as described for creating the planking on a door. If you are working in 7mm scale or larger, however, a texture will be required. A good material to replicate stucco is white gesso primer, used to prime canvas, which can be obtained from art suppliers. After painting a thin coating of gesso on the face of the card, the chasing can then be scored in to give a convincing effect.

Stringcourses and cornices will need to be added to the walls. These can be made from card, balsa or styrene strip. Before the roof is added, fix all the windows and doors into position. Since numerous windows of the distinctive, multi-paned design will be required, it might be worth looking at windows available as etchings or laser-cut versions. GT Buildings, for example, produces this type of window in 4mm scale, while True Texture has a multi-paned sash window laser-cut from card. For 7mm scale, try York Model Making's range of laser-cut frames made from styrene. Before fitting they will need painting; brass etchings will first need an undercoat before adding the top coat. The common colour for the frames would be white. To achieve the best finish use a white spray primer. Glazing should be added before fitting, using a piece of clear celluloid and spray mount. Now the window frame can be fixed into the reveals with glue or strips of double-sided tape. When the windows have been fixed, curtains can be added to the rear using tissue or crêpe paper and fixed with either glue or double-sided tape. If the windows have ornamental surrounds, these will have to be fabricated. Since a good number will be required for the model, the best way to create identical items in any number is to reproduce them as resin castings. Start by creating one moulding from scratch to use as a master, then make a box around the master to contain liquid rubber and leave this to set over a couple of days. You will now have a mould into which liquid resin can then be poured. This again will be left to harden off, resulting in a reproduction of the master. Then it is just a matter of repeating the last stage of the exercise until the required number has been made.

Turning to the rooflines, a sub-base will first need to be provided by constructing a flat top to the building. This will be positioned below any parapets running around the top of the walls and is supported by strips of card glued to the inside of the shell. The shallow pitched roofs can now be constructed on this flat base. Both types of roof profile will require a number of trusses made from card or foam board. It might be worth adding some strips to add extra support to the roof panels. The roof panels themselves can now be cut from card. Slates are cut from thin card and fixed to the panels with double-sided tape. If the roof covering consists of pantiles, it is easier to use pre-scribed or moulded styrene panels, such as those from the Wills building pack range. To finish, ridge tiles or flashing strips need to be added, as well as flashing anywhere the roof meets walls, parapets or chimney stacks. Another style of roof profile common to the Regency town house was the mansard roof, which consists of a gable roof with two angles of pitch: a steep angle from the eaves combined with a shallow angle to the ridge. This style gave extra roof space to accommodate attic rooms lit by the addition of dormers or skylights. The end walls would be built higher with copings provided. Dividing walls were also built up to the same height. Card strips used to create the copings may require a coating of filler plaster or gesso on

larger scale models. Chimney stacks complete the structure. On a mansard roof these are positioned as part of the end and dividing walls. The stacks can be built up from card with stringcourses and cornices added from strips of card. Again these are coated with gesso for a rendered finish or embossed brick styrene is used. A solution for chimney pots can be found in the white metal castings in 4mm scale from Langley and other suppliers, and in 7mm scale from S&D Models. These are secured with flaunching made from Milliput or a small amount of Das modelling clay. Before painting it is necessary to fix all the detailing. Downpipes with header hoppers made from styrene or brass rod can be fixed to the walls. Guttering would be concealed behind the parapet or cornice, so there is no need to model it. For other details that would have been in metal, such as window guards, balconies and railings, you may be able to source something close to what you are looking for from etchings supplied by Scale Link, Langley Models or other suppliers.

This Victorian town house shows the influence of the style known as Gothic Revival. The windows have distinctive pointed arches and decorative brick lintels. Another notable feature was the introduction of coloured brick in the string courses, lintels and cornices.

The front of a large middle-class Victorian town terrace from the 1860s. The availability of cheap glass made it possible to incorporate it in large bays, although these were reserved for the ground floor. This terrace includes the angled bays, together with a canopy linking the bays.

This model can easily be made in low relief and would be effective at the back of the layout up to the back scene. It will save space and create depth at the same time. However, make sure that the building is modelled just over the ridge of the roof. This will look more convincing, creating the impression of the building extending to the full depth. If the building is cut in half along the ridge it will look wrong.

VICTORIAN TOWN HOUSES AND VILLAS

Large early Victorian terraced town houses were similar to those of the preceding Regency period, although certain fashions had changed. From the 1850s the influences of foreign travel and Queen Victoria's holiday retreat at Osborne House on the Isle of Wight started a trend for affluent industrial entrepreneurs and merchants to build new town houses and villas with Italianate styling. Shallow pitched roofs with overhanging eaves now became fashionable. These were supported by brackets of stone or terracotta known as corbels. Windows were usually in pairs with round heads and rounded

brick lintels over the top. Stringcourses also featured in different coloured brick. The windows were still sash frames, although fewer panes were commonly used with no more than three panes to each sash, all with an arched top frame. Facing bricks of red and cream became popular, augmenting the stucco finish.

The Gothic Revival style, incorporating features of medieval architecture, became fashionable for houses as well as for some of the most famous British railway and public buildings. The windows were much like those of the Italianate style, although with the distinctive pointed arch. Coloured coursing was evident on the brick lintels. Roof shapes changed from a shallow pitch to a very steep pitch, decorated with shaped roofing tiles and slates. Finishes included elaborate ridge tiles and terracotta finials. The steep gables would have decorative barge-boards.

MODELLING VICTORIAN TOWN HOUSES

The construction and materials used for the shells are the same as for the Regency house (see above). The roof profile, however, has a much steeper pitch and this will require making the gable end walls to accommodate it. Other architectural differences would see larger panes used in the sash frames. The front facade of the house would have the windows contained in large bays. In the early Victorian period these bay windows were confined to the ground floor, but later the bays were often extended to the first floor. The bay walls can be made to the required shape from card. The bay projected out from the main front wall with its sides set at an angle of 45 degrees. The brickwork was extended at the corners to support the lintel and roof on the ground-floor bay; this was repeated if a first-floor bay was included. Sometimes stone mullion pillars were used as a support rather than the corner brickwork. By cutting out the window apertures from the card the corners can be left in situ. Before the bays are fitted, a large aperture will have to be cut out of the main wall. The best method is to complete the bays as separate units with all the window frames and curtains fitted to the inside. Fit the sills, lintels

Typical row of brick terraced railway company houses fronting Martin Nield's pre-grouping layout 'Eccleston'.

and roof to the ground-floor bay, with any styrene embossed brick already added. The bays can then be fitted up to the walls. The joints, especially where the bay joins up, will need a little Das modelling clay as filler. The brick courses can then be scribed in when dry to complete the join. For the window frames I would suggest using brass etchings or laser-cut ones. Some of the bays featured terracotta mouldings and corbels to support the sills and lintels. To model these details, a master should be made and then a mould taken from this. Using the mould a number of castings can made to use on the model. Slates or tiles should be added to the roof, with lead flashings to all the joins. Decorative tiles and slates with shaped edges were sometimes used, both on the bay and the main roof.

During the 1870s and 1880s towers and turrets became a popular addition to the end of a terrace. These could be square, round or octagonal in shape. Octagonal towers might have a wraparound window that spread around up to four or even five sides. The tower or turret would generally be topped by a conical spire with slates or tiles, again with decora-

tive shapes being used. The corner edges would have lead flashings to the seams and the top of the spire would be finished with a terracotta finial. Some spires were clad in lead, zinc or copper sheet, notably when other styles, such as the popular bell-shaped cap, replaced the cone. Towers and turrets can be modelled in the same way as the bay windows, with care taken on the wraparound window and the spire. The latter might benefit from the use of thin metal foil to create the lead flashing or sheeting. The bell-shaped cap might be a problem, although one solution might be to sculpt it from modelling clay.

A few kits and off-the shelf models of these buildings available on the market include low relief samples in card from Bilt-eezi, Superquick and Metcalfe. Ready-made samples in Bachmann's Scenecraft range include a row of low-relief Victorian tenements that show the rear of the terrace. A facade in Regency style is listed as a solicitor's office or doctor's surgery. There is also a section of a Victorian terrace with a single ground-floor bay window; a number of these models can be joined to make a longer terrace if required.

LEFT: *A typical mid-Victorian middle-class terrace facade. Note the large bay window to the ground-floor front parlour and the use of different coloured bricks as decoration above the door and up to the eaves. The ridge tile decoration terminates with terracotta finials on the gable end of the main roof and the dormer.*

BELOW: *The construction of a typical angled bay window: (A) the components that need to be cut from card to make up the basic structure; (B) adding the hipped roof panel sections and the windowsills; (C) the completed structure with the sash windows fitted from behind and the tile or slate roof covering in place.*

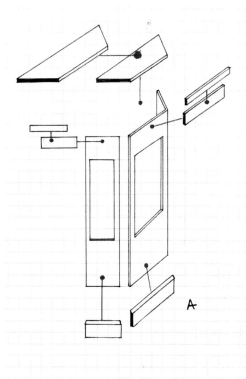

A

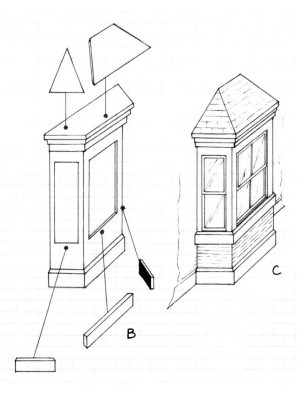

B

C

A STARTER PROJECT TO BUILD AN OUTHOUSE

Until the 1960s most commercial and domestic housing in our towns and cities would feature some kind of outhouse. This usually consisted of the outside toilet or 'privy', a coal house and sometimes a wash house. I have decided to include a project to build one of these once-common buildings as a starter model. Although this particular building has been constructed from stone, there is no reason why the same example could not be built from brick. My advice would be to use an outer skin of embossed styrene brick sheet. The cutting, applying and painting of this material is described in Chapter 1 and the painting in Chapter 5.

This model will provide the ideal project for any modeller starting out to try and create an urban model railway. At the same time it will give others the opportunity to add an extra building to the back yards of their existing models.

The sides and gable ends are all cut from mounting card. Note the angled cut-away sections from the gable ends have been saved to use as corner bracing.

The walls, ends and floor are all assembled together using an impact adhesive such as Bostik.

The lintels and sills are added from a strip of the same mounting card, before the walls are given a skin of Das modelling clay.

Before moving onto the scribing stage it is worth cleaning up all the door and window reveals with a small file.

The next stage was to scribe out all the stonework, starting with the corner quoins. Always follow

photographs of the prototype to achieve the best results.

In this photograph the window frame has already been cut from card. I attached double-sided tape to the rear of the card before cutting out. The matt facing side of the card is coloured using a Pro-Marker pen.

All the window frames and doors are made from the same thin card – I used old greetings cards. These were all then fixed into the door and window apertures.

Before adding the roof I decided to paint the stonework. I started with the mortar first, using a thin wash of Naples Yellow oil paint. The final stone effect was dry brushed using colours mixed on the palette, replicating the prototype as close as possible.

The next stage was to mark out all the tiles to roof this building. I used a square grid supplied on the graphics software on my computer, which was not far away from the size of tiles required for this model.

The next task was to cut them all out individually using one square for the tile and one square for the over-lap.

The roof sub-base has been added using two panels of the same mounting card that was used to construct the walls.

With the sub-base complete, the cut-out tiles can be fixed into

position. Start the first row along the eaves and overlap each row of tiles until the ridge has been reached.

This photograph shows the tiling nearly completed. All the tiles were fixed to the sub-base using double-sided tape.

The roof has now been tiled completely and just needs the ridge tiles to be fixed. Note how the tiles have purposely been fixed slightly out of line with each other; his was to achieve a more rustic and authentic look to the roof.

The next stage was to give the roof a coat of base colour. I used Humbrol Matt Tank Grey in the spray form to give an overall flat finish. You must first mask the painted walls off.

This photograph reveals the effect of dry-brush painting some of the individual tiles and the weathering applied, including the lichen growth. All this was achieved by using oil paint and mixing the colours on a palette first.

I decided to add some plant growth on the building. I used one of the Woodland Scenics foliage mats for this, which was attached the corner of the building using spray mount.

The finished model, with a chimney stack added to the wash house. This was constructed from off-cuts of mounting card. Das clay was added and scribed in the same way as the walls, and to finish a white metal cast chimney pot was added from the Langley Models range.

MILL WORKERS' AND VICTORIAN TERRACES

The housing built by textile mill owners for their workers sometimes included attic rooms for weavers to work from home. Most, however, were fairly basic with either one room up and one down, or two up and two down. Mill towns like Belper in Derbyshire had streets with rows of terraces. Housing of this type was also provided for other industries. Not so far away from Belper is Ironville, where the Butterley Company built similar rows as an 'industrial model village' to house those who worked in its iron foundries. Other 'model villages' sprang up

A row of three-storey mill-workers' houses, built by Thomas Evans at Darley Abbey.

A closer view of the cottages illustrates their rendered finish.

In contrast, these workers' cottages in 'Poplar Row' are left unrendered.

Close-up of stone terraces provided by Jedediah Strutt for his mill workers in Belper, Derbyshire.

The three-storey weavers' cottages at Lea Mills date from the first half of the eighteenth century.

A row of ironworkers' houses originally built by Richard Crawshay at Rhyd-y-car, Merthyr Tydfil, at the end of the eighteenth century. They have been reconstructed at St Fagans National History Museum, near Cardiff.

This close-up of one of the Rhyd-y-car houses illustrates the cramped living accommodation, with one room up and one down.

Stone Row was built by the Butterley Company to house the families of ironworkers at Ironville, Derbyshire. Housing developments such as these, where companies also provided for their workers' educational and recreational needs, became known as Model Villages.

all over the country. Local stone was used for most of the early terraces, but brick was employed when it became more readily available. The favoured material to roof these houses was Welsh slate and typical sash windows were fitted. Developments to serve the industrial towns took over vast areas of land, with the owners providing other amenities as well

A typical brick-built Victorian terrace with large four-paned sash windows.

The ground floor of a millworker's cottage in West Yorkshire. Note the basement floor to this building, requiring steps to reach the front door.

The front of a row of gritstone mill houses, again in West Yorkshire. The dark weathering to the stonework is common in this part of the Pennines.

The Midland Railway terrace in Derby, built by the railway company in 1842 to house its workers. These red-brick houses stand on stone plinths with stone door cases, string courses and cornices. A parapet extension to the front wall conceals the low gabled roof.

as housing. The railway companies also provided this style of housing for the workers at their massive locomotive and rolling stock works. Towns like Brighton, Swindon, Crewe, Doncaster and Derby all grew with the coming of the railways. The railway companies provided for their workers' every need, including good quality housing stock. All of their buildings were given architectural details and decoration intended to emphasize the company's importance. This was even extended to the workers' houses. The railway cottages outside Derby station, built by the Midland Railway Company, have been restored to their former glory and are now desirable and expensive properties within the modern city.

This view of the Midland Railway terrace shows the use of stone for the door cases and other decoration. Note the string course separating the storeys and the twelve-paned sash windows.

Sheffield Place, a cul-de-sac provided in a break in the terrace row. Like the main terrace, this has been sympathetically restored to its former glory and has become very desirable property for professionals in Derby.

The front of the brick-built mill-workers' terrace in Belper.

This stone-built, two-storey mill-workers' terrace in West Yorkshire is of a type common in this part of the country. Note how the roofline follows the slope of the hillside. The deep wall area between the lintel of the first-floor windows and the roofline would accommodate loft rooms. Since there were full windows only on the gable ends of the terrace, the rooms in between depended on light and ventilation from roof lights.

This end-of-terrace pub has been fitted with snow boards to protect the glass roof of the conservatory underneath.

A more detailed view showing the snow boards in position just above the gutters. The chimney stack is notable for its two Queen pots.

The rear of the mill-workers' cottages in Belper. Note the narrow linear gardens provided for growing vegetables and perhaps for keeping chickens.

The extensions to the backs of the Midland Railway terraces would provide a scullery on the ground floor and a back bedroom above.

This view of the back of Short Row in Belper gives a good impression of these cottages' brickwork. Note the four-paned sash window to the upper floor.

A three-storey brick-built terrace. The building style and window detail is exactly the same as that of the single-storey cottage, retaining the identity of the owners.

MODELLING VICTORIAN TERRACE HOUSES

Numerous kits and off-the-shelf models of Victorian terraces have been available on the model railway market over the years, probably because this type of house was built in such great numbers. Indeed, this style of building, although with modern improvements, can still be seen in nearly every British town and city. The Victorian terrace is also associated with the railway, with rows of them backing onto the tracks in urban areas.

Between them Bilt-eezi, Superquick, Howard Scenics and Metcalfe, all with one or two models, can supply a comprehensive range of card kits, while Wills Finecast includes a kit in their plastic building range. Now there are resin models available on the market, especially those from Hornby and Bachmann. Both companies have produced a number of variations on the humble terrace. I have

The standard layout for a Victorian terrace house was for the scullery to be added to the rear as a lean-to extension. This would be just on the ground floor on the early buildings, but later the extension would be taken up to the roof eaves, creating a first floor for extra accommodation, usually as a back bedroom. This extension would be divided into half and shared with the next property in the terrace.

The corner of the railway terrace in Derby would originally have been a pub. The entrance has been sympathetically incorporated as a special feature to this property's ground floor.

The railway terrace houses that did not face the main thoroughfare were not provided with stone embellishments intended to impress the masses going to and from the station.

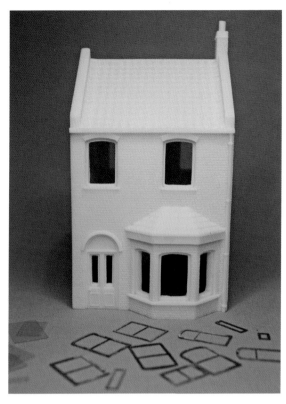

A finished, but unpainted, single terrace house available from the Hornby Skaledale range of resin cast buildings. Models of this type may appeal to modellers who wish to do something creative, even if it is only painting and fitting the windows.

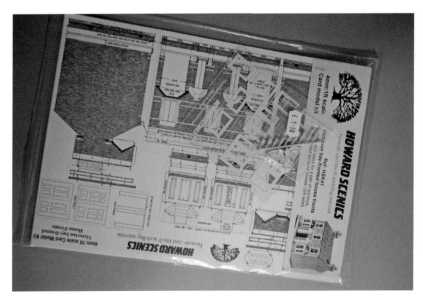

A basic card kit of two brick-built terrace houses available from Howard Scenics.

The first stage was to give the resin casting a spray coat of red acrylic matt primer as a base to the brick colour.

The etched brass window frames supplied were also given a spray of undercoat with yellow matt primer.

included here details of a resin sample from Hornby that requires painting. This is a very good casting, but you will still have to use your skills to paint and finish the model.

The finished, painted model, with the windows fixed into position. The brickwork was given a wash of pale cream oil paint, brushed on all over and letting it flow freely into all the mortar gaps. The surface was then wiped clean with a kitchen towel, leaving the paint where it was required. The next stage involved dry brushing the walls and terracotta roof tiles with toned-down Indian Red applied over the raised surface of the brickwork and the tiles. A few bricks and tiles were picked out in light chrome orange and brown before blending with a very dry brush to give the final effect. Weathering was also added and the window frames were painted a dark green.

EDWARDIAN HOUSES

The Edwardian period was one of great political and social change that brought a new era for the domestic housing scene. As the wealth of the nation increased, there was a serious attempt to create new welfare schemes to solve the housing problems of the working class. Work started on clearing the older slum terraces of one up and one down, where families of six or more were living under one roof, and replacing them with cheaper, but larger houses.

ROOF PITCH ESTIMATED AT. 30°   GRADIENT. 5°.

The dimensions of this brick-built mill-workers' terrace can be estimated by comparing the known dimensions of a door with other features as they appear on a photograph.

The rear arrangement of terraced houses: (left) the early arrangement with just a ground-floor scullery at the back; (right) the later design with the scullery on the ground floor and a back bedroom accommodated in the first floor above. The red line indicates the division between the properties.

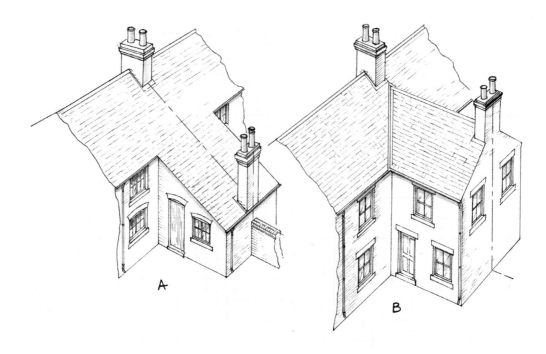

A

B

Developments spread even further out into the rural land surrounding the towns and cities, creating the suburbs. This period would even see new towns established in regions that would later be designated as green belt land. The first of these was Letchworth, Hertfordshire, which became known as a Garden City, These developments created havens for the middle classes, who could now commute into the cities by train to work but live in a semi-rural environment.

The first houses built in this period started to take shape in the 1890s. Initially they were still under the architectural influence of what had gone before. The spread of the suburban rail network and cheaper tickets meant that the middle classes could now live further out of town where more land was available. The new houses could offer gardens for relaxation that provided a little piece of the countryside on your doorstep. The working class could also afford to move away from the slums that had become synonymous with smoky industrial towns, settling in small suburban terraces that offered more accommodation and even gave them their own privy, instead of sharing one with the neighbours.

Some large companies began to build special model villages for their workers using the new forms of housing and providing plenty of green areas, landscaped to replicate an impression of the countryside. Bournville, established by the Cadbury family, and Lever Brothers' Port Sunlight are two developments that were totally built for their workers; they became, and remain, very desirable areas in which to live.

Most houses were being built taller and deeper than before, with as much attention paid to the rear of the property as the front. The exterior style of suburban housing reflected the Old English and Queen Anne Revival styles promoted by architects such as Norman Shaw. This gave rise to a new vogue in house style closely aligned to the Arts and Crafts movement. Pebble-dash rendering became a fashionable covering for the walls, while the gable fronts were finished with black-and-white mock half-timbering. Mock half-timbering also became popular for finishing the front of gables, together with hanging terracotta tiles. Other uses for terracotta decoration

included decorative tiles in the porch and hallways, reviving those of upper-class villas of earlier periods. What resulted was a general mix of previous styles, from Tudor and Jacobean, through Georgian and Regency to Gothic Revival. These styles were also to be found on high street shop facades and on public buildings. Neo-Georgian embellishments became common. At the same time as this historicist movement held sway over architecture, some architects during the 1890s and 1900s introduced elements of Art Nouveau, a new trend that rejected historicism. One feature that achieved some popularity was the use of stained glass in leaded top lights and doors.

The Edwardian period also saw the development of the semi-detached house, which became a very popular style saving space and money, while still giving some of the feeling that a detached house would provide.

MODELLING THE EDWARDIAN HOUSE

This style of house offers a vast amount of opportunity, both in techniques and materials, if you choose to build from scratch. There are many buildings of this type that you can measure for the preparation of a drawing. Indeed, there is a good chance that you may be living in just such a building.

As usual, the shells can be built from card, ensuring there is sufficient bracing at the corners and between the outer walls. To create a brick skin to the building I would recommend using pre-scribed styrene sheet, as before. In order to replicate a pebble-dash finish I have two suggestions. The first involves stippling No More Cracks plaster filler, supplied by Unibond, onto the face of card that has been given a coating of PVA. The effect achieved will look better in the larger scales. The second method is to sieve pepper over the wet PVA. This may sound unlikely, but the effect can look very convincing and works well on 4mm models or smaller. It is always a good idea to paint this before adding the windows. Photographs should give you an idea of the authentic colours used for the period of your model. The window frames can be cut from card, but brass etchings from GT Models or card laser-cut frames from True Texture might be a better alternative. Clear glazing can be easily obtained from scrap packaging, but stained glass and coloured panels might prove a problem. You could try to colour them yourself using Staedtler Lumocolor permanent marker pens. Pre-printed acetate sheets by Langley Models intended for church windows would be fine for 4mm scale or lower. The bay window was again very popular, with angled corners extended up to the roof line and capped with a mock half-timbered gable. Another window feature that became common on larger middle-class semi-detached houses was the introduction of French windows on the ground floor at the rear of the house; they were also sometimes inserted on the first floor at the front, combined with a balcony. All these features are available as brass etchings or laser-cut samples.

Doors can be made up from card with two or three vertical panels at the bottom and multiple or just one pane of glass in the top panel, sometimes with a shaped top and glazed with the same coloured glass patterns as the top lights to the windows. The entrance porch was another distinctive feature, with the earlier middle-class houses having ornate perforated woodwork and wooden spindles. Later examples, influenced by Art Deco in the 1920s, had a semicircular top with the porch actually set into the front wall.

The roofs of Edwardian houses were generally covered with terracotta tiles, some of which, on certain rows, had shaped edges. Laser-cut samples in various shapes are available from York Modelmaking. There is also an embossed terracotta tiled plastic sheet available in the Wills builders packs that includes shaped tiles. The only problems I have with these are the restricted size of the sheet and the thickness of the plastic, which makes cutting rather difficult. The front gables above the front bay windows are often very prominent, overhanging the main walls and the bay, and are supported on wooden brackets. The facades to these bays were faced with mock-Tudor timbering, usually painted to give the 'traditional' black-and-white finish. Otherwise, decorative tile hanging was used here and to face the bay walls between the windows. Both the timber-clad and tile-hung gables were finished with barge-boards. The

roofs to the gables would use the same tiles as the main roof covering, complete with ridge tiles and a terracotta finial to add that extra decoration to the apex of the gable.

The chimney stacks were built of brick, although sometimes the pebble-dashing was extended onto them. The stepped brickwork at the top of the chimney was often supported by brick corbels. Both plain round chimney pots and those with square crowned tops were used. Examples for use on a model are available from suppliers such as Langley Models in 4mm scale and from S&D Models for any 7mm requirements.

THE 1930s HOUSE

The years between the wars were turbulent, but there were great advances in technology. Electricity became available to light domestic homes for the first time. The quest for speed and luxury was very evident in all forms of transport, with great competition between rival companies and countries. Ocean liners competed to be the fastest across the Atlantic Ocean and to be rewarded the prestigious Blue Riband. The railways also reached their heyday before the Second World War would bring them nearly to breaking point. This was a period of luxury trains with glamorous names and fierce competition between the big four companies to claim speed records. The era also saw the birth of air travel. Its expense meant that it remained the preserve of the wealthy, but airliners started to appear in the skies over Britain. All this modernization was reflected in urban buildings as the simple geometrical lines and patterns of Art Deco design appeared on the high street and in homes.

Despite the turbulent financial markets, huge numbers of houses were built in this decade, mostly in the suburbs around London and other major cities. The period would see the creation of large building companies aided by government incentives to build houses for the masses. Cheap land prices made feasible the rise of large estates comprising the characteristic avenues, crescents and cul-de-sacs flanked by the archetypal semi. A concurrent low-cost housing

An early bungalow design. Bungalow living started to be popular in the inter-war years. Note the use of gables finished with decorative barge-boards and the semicircular front porch, which were to become common features of the 1930s house.

The basic design for the family detached house, as seen here, was built in the thousands and became the standard house of middle-class suburbia.

boom would see the emergence of council estates of houses built to the semi-detached format or as short terraces, each with about four houses. Large estates were built around the suburbs and housing of this type even made an appearance in rural areas to give low-cost homes to all the working classes.

The exteriors of these houses were influenced by the architects who had worked under the banner of the Arts and Crafts movements a few decades before. C.F.A. Voysey, M.H. Baillie Scott and Edwin Lutyens had all made their mark introducing mock-Tudor, Neo-Georgian and pseudo-Elizabethan embellishments to the standard plain box semi or detached houses. Now, however, a number of houses started to appear in the suburbs that owed more to the Modern Movement, influenced by the

The semi-detached version of this type of house, again using a semicircular porch, can be seen in the suburbs of any large British town or city.

Hollywood films that brought glamour into people's lives. This streamlined American version of Art Deco introduced the familiar sunray patterns of coloured glass and curved metal-framed bay windows. It was also to be seen in the industrial factories and railway architecture of the period.

The most common style to emerge over this period was undoubtedly the semi-detached house or bungalow with curved bay windows and overhanging gables at the front. It would have a semicircular-topped porch and a square centrally positioned chimney on a steeply pitched, red-tiled hipped roof. I always think of them as 'Bayko' houses, named after the construction toy I remember from my childhood. Detached houses in this style were the same, but without the mirror image. Most of them, especially those built for the middle classes, had a garage alongside or built on to provide for the family cars that were starting to appear once the likes of Morris and Austin had made them affordable.

The *Style moderne* or Art Deco lines to the houses echo those of the glamorous ocean liners. The footprint was more or less the same, but the main difference came in the form of sleek bay windows with long landscape panes of glass mounted in metal frames with a distinctive curve at the ends. The top one would have a central rectangular hinged light with clear and coloured chevron or sun-rise patterns set into lead. The doors were also modern in design with a tall vertical pane of glass, also with the chevron or sunray design. The porch, however, would give way to simpler designs with a stepped and recessed surround capped with a single flat concrete porch hood extended into the bottom front bay. The first-floor bay had an extended parapet with a flat top intended to give the impression of a flat roof to the building and mask the hipped roof behind it. The corner window on the first floor could be extended to wrap around the actual corner in order to continue the sleek appearance. Some houses had a roof that was totally flat rather than the traditional steeply pitched and hipped type, replicating the deco houses across the Atlantic in Miami and the cities on the West Coast.

A pebble-dashed finish or the finer plaster render of stucco was still employed. Lines were added in slight relief to the walls to extend the influence of liner design seen in the windows and other features. In imitation of American examples, the buildings were painted bright white with sky blue lines added, although it was rare for the bright white facade to stand out against an ultramarine sky as it would in Miami.

THE 1960s AND MODERN HOUSING

There was a great need for housing after the Second World War. The London Blitz and the extensive bombing raids over the major towns and cities had destroyed thousands of homes. The answer to the campaign to provide temporary housing was the prefabricated bungalow, popularly known as the prefab. These were designed so that they could be built quickly and in large numbers: more than 155,000

There was a great need for temporary housing after the devastation of the Second World War. The answer was the prefab bungalow, popularly known as 'tin palaces'. These were manufactured off-site and erected on a prepared foundation with services ready to be connected. This sample has been rebuilt as part of the collection at St Fagans National History Museum.

The chalet style – half house, half bungalow – became popular in the 1970s. The steep pitch to the roof was intended to accommodate attic or dormer rooms, as they became known. There would be an extended dormer window to the front and sometimes also to the rear.

prefab bungalows were built in Britain, as well as a number of two-storey prefabricated houses. Although they were only intended as a short-term measure to cover the housing shortage, many of these houses were lived in throughout the 1950s and well into the 1960s. A few still survive today. The buildings were constructed using aluminium frames and panels and were fabricated on production lines that had supplied aircraft during the war. The type B2 bungalow was made up of four pre-assembled sections that came complete with all the necessary plumbing, gas and pipework. Each section was transported to the intended location and lifted onto a pre-prepared brick foundation. The sections were then bolted together and all the joints sealed. Once the services were connected it was ready for occupation. Type B2 prefabs soon became known affectionately as 'tin palaces'.

The early 1950s would also see the building of council houses, some of which too were built in sections. The extensive building plans drawn up included the creation of massive council estates principally comprising semi-detached houses, although again short terraces would also be built. At the end of the 1950s there were calls for councils to turn

to high-rise living. The rows of Victorian terraces and tenements were demolished in a frenzy of slum clearance. New prefabricated council estates were built in the sky. One of the first was the Park Hill Flats (1957–61) in Sheffield; these were Grade II* listed in 1998 and, unlikely many other developments, have recently been renovated. During the early 1960s tower blocks containing council flats became a common sight in the suburbs of industrial towns and cities.

The bungalow, which was introduced a few decades before, became popular again. Most detached domestic property would be built to the box style, using large panes of glass to glaze the windows. Picture windows became very popular during the late 1950s and the fashion lasted into the early 1970s. Opening lights would be provided at the sides or above the large panes. Council housing would also adapt picture windows for use in new properties. Another trend in the 1970s was for the chalet design of bungalow, utilizing a steeply pitched roof that would accommodate upstairs rooms fitted with dormer windows. The result, a cross between a bungalow and a house,

Revival styles were common in the new builds of the 1980s. The country cottage was evoked by the use of mock-Tudor half-timbered fronts, tile-hung gables and barge-boards, which became fashionable again. Georgian windows and mock-leaded lights also reflected period architecture, but were just set-dressing to the standard brick and blockwork box.

became affectionately known as the 'dormer'. During the 1980s fashions turned back towards traditional styles as the popular expectation and vision of the perfect house once more reflected the image of the country cottage. Developers have tried to meet this need in the standard family house, although for the most part it was just set-dressing on the basic box. The building would be built using cavity walls, with an inner skin of blockwork and an outer skin of brick. Builders would then add traditional dressings, such as mock half-timbering and hanging tiles; even thatched roofs were used on some executive homes. The return to mock decoration is not new, of course, as it was popular in the 1920s and 1930s. Since the late 1970s nearly all our domestic houses have been converted to benefit from double glazing. The traditional wooden single-glazed units have been ripped out and replaced, initially with aluminium frames and more recently with uPVC. These can look totally out of place in Victorian and Edwardian properties unless they have been sympathetically designed to replicate the old frames. This has been extended to replacing doors with plastic imitations, which again can look awful on older properties. Other additions have seen satellite dishes strapped to the sides of chimney stacks, and more recently solar panels covering the roof.

The domestic housing presently being built seems to be a mishmash of styles. The traditional designs are still in vogue, but they are generally mixed up with the modern. The modern family house has had to accommodate our love affair with the car. Houses being built today seem to make this a priority, with a house built over a double garage. Older domestic properties have also been adapted to the needs of the car, with traditional front gardens paved over or tarmacked to make car parks. While compiling this book I have become more aware of this development, as it is just about impossible to take a photograph of any house, or other building for that matter, without a car getting in the way.

So we come to the future. The need for housing to cater for an ever growing population is again a major problem to the government. Every day we hear about the thousands of new houses that need to be built, but we will have to wait and see what styles and designs are adopted. Over the next few decades we may see the adoption of a trend towards eco living, as the need to develop sustainable energy gains in importance. I am sure, however, that the vernacular tradition will be retained, while cutting-edge technology is exploited in a highly integrated way to meet modern life styles.

MODELLING THE DOMESTIC URBAN HOUSE: FROM THE VICTORIAN TERRACE TO THE MODERN ERA

After the above outline of the development of the domestic house since the eighteenth century, it is now time to look at how to make models of them and what is available to the modeller as kits or off-the-shelf samples. There is a vast amount of kits and ready-made models of terrace houses on the market. This is probably because this type of housing was often related to the railways and was to be found backing onto railway lines in urban areas. The problem with kits and 'ready-to-plant' models is that they only come as individual or twin units. If you want to build up a terrace you will have to purchase a good number and join them up. It might be easier and cheaper to build the terrace as a whole unit from scratch.

MODELLING VICTORIAN TERRACES FROM SCRATCH

As with any modelling project, you should start by obtaining the information required to build the model. It would help if you can arrange a visit to measure up, but with a terrace this might not be possible. I would suggest taking photographs of one or two together in the row and use these to calculate your measurements, based on those of a feature that you can measure accurately, such as a window or a door. You will stand a better chance of acquiring accurate measurements if you can take a photograph from a position as straight on as possible. Print out a copy of the photograph and mark lines across it, taking in the windows, doors and any other exterior features. Starting with the feature you have accurately measured, you can then estimate all the other measurements. This won't be totally accurate, but will be good enough for the model. With this information down on paper, the rest of the terrace can then be calculated as you just need to repeat the first measurements taken.

A scale drawing can now be produced from this information to the scale of your finished model. I would recommend using mounting card for the shell, although thinner foam board could be used. Transfer your drawing by redrawing it onto the chosen material. The next stage is to cut everything out, remembering that it is easier to cut out the window and door apertures first. I would also advise leaving a little extra added to the baseline to give the terrace some footings. Once the walls have been cut out, add the styrene embossed brick to the model, making sure that the corners line up and that the window and door apertures are cut away. If the terrace is built from stone or has a rendered finish, this can be applied when the walls have been fixed together.

The embossed styrene-covered sides are then assembled together. The covering overlapping on the front and back walls can be trimmed off to give a clean joint, although the mortar courses will need to be carried around the corner. This can be carried out by using a fine needle file. A little cleaning and filler will also be required to give a convincing result to the corner.

The stone of rendered finish can be produced using Das modelling clay and No More Cracks plaster filler. When scribing out the stonework to replicate the stone of the prototype, always remember to refer to photographs.

The next stage is to add windows and doors to the model. These can be cut from card, with clear celluloid glazing material assembled into the frames. Alternatively, you could opt to use etched or laser-cut frames, which are available from True Texture and other firms. Doors also come in etched form or as laser-cut samples, but they are reasonably easy to construct from card in the way described in the diagrams.

The roof's substructure is built from mounting card and then covered with slates or tiles. On some terrace rows the roofline is concealed behind a parapet extension to the front wall. This is evident on the typical London terrace and the Midland Railway workers' terraces at Derby, illustrated earlier.

To finish the roof, chimney stacks are added using mounting card, which is covered with styrene if they are built from brick. Apply the same technique to the corners of the stacks as have been used for corners to the main walls. The stacks will need chimney pots and flaunching to finish. Chimney pots may be had as white metal castings from Langley Models, from Shire Scenes in 4mm scale and from S&D Models in 7mm scale. Other roofline details, such as guttering and downpipes, can be made from styrene rod or strip supplied by companies such as Evergreen.

Before the model is complete it will need painting and weathering. Full details of the necessary techniques will be found in Chapter 5.

KITS AND OFF-THE-SHELF MODELS

As I mentioned earlier, there are a few kits available if you are daunted by the thought of building from scratch. Victorian terrace houses are available in card from Bilt-eezi, Superquick, Metcalfe and Howard Scenics. Off-the-shelf samples are included in Hornby's Skaledale and Bachmann's Scenecraft ranges, as well as from other sources. One of the resin castings from Hornby, which comes unpainted and with etched windows that need to be fitted, is illustrated earlier to show how it can be painted and finished to make a convincing model.

Semis and detached houses from the 1930s are again catered for with card kits from Bilt-eezi, Superquick and Metcalfe. A few plastic models in these styles, taken from the original dies produced by Airfix, are marketed by Dapol. Both Hornby's Skaledale and Bachmann's Scenecraft ranges include ready-made models of 1930s semis and detached houses. Both also cover modern detached houses: an interesting variant available from Bachmann shows a house under construction. There are also card kits of modern houses and council houses.

CHAPTER THREE

COMMERCIAL AND SERVICE BUILDINGS

One way of bringing some individuality to terrace housing is to set it in context with other buildings that served the residents. The archetypal terraced street for many British television viewers appears in 'Coronation Street', where the terrace has a corner shop at one end and a public house at the other.

URBAN PUBLIC HOUSES

Most back-street public houses resembled something not unlike the Rover's Return of 'Coronation Street'. There was accommodation upstairs and to the back of the building, while the front ground floor of the building comprised a public bar and lounge bar or snug. Below that there would be a basement cellar for storing and keeping the beer. Most of the pubs would feature fairly large windows with decorative frames, lintels and sills. The glazing would often have frosted panes into which the name of the pub or brewery was etched. Depending on the size of the pub and its importance, the brewery would

Close-up of the corner, showing the panel and the lettering style used.

The terrace corner public house at Blists Hill Victorian Town shows the use of the entrance on the angled corner wall. The panel above the door has been used to promote the names of the pub and the brewery.

The wedge-shaped Brunswick Inn, with its curved end, was built for the railway workers in Derby as part of the Midland Railway's housing outside the station. Note the high side walls with a parapet in front of the roof, extending on three sides of the building. The pub has been restored to its former glory and has its own micro-brewery incorporated on the ground floor.

Dwarfed by the building next to it, this town pub stands on Station Street in Burton upon Trent. Note the unusual facing wall given to this Victorian ale house.

The Coopers Tavern, a typical town pub that has survived in its original form.

The Red Lion Hotel once stood in Burslem, but has now been rebuilt as part of the street scene at Crich Tramway Village. The ornate use of decorative ceramics on pub facades was once common and can still be seen in many towns and cities.

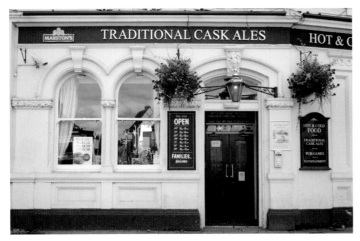

A good example of a Victorian town pub facade. Round-topped windows, combined with ornate cornices, were a popular feature.

Another round-topped window, here encased in decorative wood panelling.

A general view of the Leopard Inn illustrates how the decorative work has been continued around the corner of this town pub. The front parapet proudly displays the name of Charrington's Fine Ales in gold letters.

supply very ornate decoration to the tiled facade, especially on town centre and city pubs.

During the 1920s and 1930s new pubs were built to serve the ever growing suburbs. The new fashions of the era were reflected in the architecture and large public houses were built in the Art Deco style, using slick lines and angles on the building's exterior. This would be extended to the interior, with an open plan area now served by one central bar. Metal-framed windows were used that featured long multiple panes. The display of the brewery's name and logo was also adapted to modern design with neon lighting giving the building a brash identity. These styles were also to be seen in towns and city centres.

In recent years the public house has tended to revert to the traditional styles. Alongside the growing interest in drinking real ales, the traditional town public house has made a comeback, together with all its associated decoration and artefacts. Unfortunately, however, it has not all been good news. The urban public house has suffered greatly from ever growing costs and the availability of cheaper alcohol from supermarkets and other licensed outlets. The boarded-up pub is now a common sight on the high streets and back streets of every town.

Another town pub with decorative wood panelling encasing the round-topped front windows. Also note the decorative cornice and the pillars between the panelled sections. The upper floor's combination of one and two storeys would make this an interesting variation for a model.

MAKING AND FIXING A SASH WINDOW FOR A LOW RELIEF MODEL PUB

The flat frontage of the 7mm low-relief model of a town public house, ready for the sash windows to be fitted.

This picture shows the frame completely cut out. You will need to be careful at this stage: always use a new, sharp blade, and make sure you cut the material in a series of cuts, rather than trying to cut through in one go.

To paint and colour the window frame, I used a Pro-Marker pen, which gave me better control than trying to paint it with a brush. The ink from the pen soaks into the card and the paper, but is repelled from the glazing material.

This photograph shows the cutting-out of the inner edge to the window frame. It is much easier to cut this out first.

The glazing was added using a clear piece of packaging. This was fixed into position using the double-sided tape that had been applied before final cutting out. The glazing bars have also been added. I used very thin strips of self-adhesive paper, the sort you find on gummed labels. You need to be very careful when cutting these, and again don't be tempted to try and cut then in one go.

The window frame is cut from thin card – I used an old Christmas card. Once the aperture had been cut I put some strips of double sided tape onto the reverse side, before cutting the outer edge out.

The next stage was to fix the top sash into the outer frame of the window reveal. Use a small amount of superglue to make the fixing.

Both the sash frames fixed into the window reveal.

This close-up image of the window clearly shows how the top sash must be fixed in, slightly overlapping the bottom sash, to give the impression that one will slide over the other.

MAKING CORBELS

A feature that you will see on most urban buildings is corbelling. This is usually a decorative addition to support a cornice or decorative string coursing on the walls. In the larger-scale models these can be made, although because you will need a good number, it is better to try to reproduce them from one master.

of the prototype. This has then been glued to a backing cut from styrene sheet. Walls have been also cut from the sheet and fixed to the backing to make a box. Liquid silicon rubber was then poured into this and allowed to set. When dry this was eased away from the box to give the mould required.

clean the casting up with a knife and file, as the resin produces a little flash especially if too much resin has been poured into the mould.

This picture shows the corbels fitted into position, supporting and adding decoration to a cornice for a Victorian building.

The master has been carved from styrene strip to the shape

The mould can now be used to pour liquid resin into and create lots of corbels. You will have to

This typical end-of-terrace pub in Burton upon Trent shows the use of white stucco walls with the stone quoins, sills and lintels picked out in black.

HOTELS

The hotel or inn has been part of the urban scene since the days of the stagecoach, providing over-night accommodation for the traveller, together with food and drink. Inns would also provide livery for the horses and garaging for the carriages. In the mid-nineteenth century the rival railway com-panies built lavish hotels combined with or near their principal stations. No expense was spared as a means to impress their clientele, including highly decorative facades that usually featured the railway company's coat of arms or logo. The entrances would be adorned with columns in the classical orders and decorative cornices. The lavish exte-rior was reflected in the interior, where the lobby might have a sweeping staircase to offer the guests a grand access to the floors and rooms above. As further emphasis, the hotels were also named after the railway company, for example The Midland, The Great Western and The North Eastern. Other hotels in towns and city centres were given the same treatment and their names, such as The Grand and The Royal, were designed to promote a feeling of elegance and opulence.

Modern hotels are built for the luxury market, but there is also a need to cater for the traveller on business and for families. This has given rise to chain hotels of a standardized design being built in town centres or on the edge close to business parks, railway stations or airports.

MODELLING URBAN PUBLIC HOUSES AND HOTELS

Card kits of the terrace corner pub are available from Superquick and Metcalfe, while 'ready-to-plant' samples may be had in Bachmann's Scenecraft range. There is also a card kit of a hotel from Superquick.

If you want to build a corner terrace pub from scratch, use the same materials and techniques as described for the basic terrace row. The only changes you will need to make are to the windows and entrance/door. The ground-floor windows will usually be larger than the normal sash design. Etched or card laser-cut windows are available from Truetexture. The frosted glazing of the bottom half of the windows can be replicated by spray mount-ing tracing paper onto the glazing. Another way to achieve this is to mask the top half of the clear glazing with masking tape and then spray the exposed half with matt varnish. Decorated glazed tiles can be replicated by using gloss printer paper, if possible choosing sheets with an adhesive back. Print panels of the tile colours onto the paper. Grout lines can be scratched into this using the tip of a scalpel blade. You could also try using glossy magazine print,

For this 7mm scale model of a back-street pub, foam board was used for the shell and the sash windows were cut from card. The walls were coated in plaster filler to replicate the rendered finish of the prototype. The roof slates were cut from old Christmas cards, with chimney pots from the S&D range of white-metal architectural components.

Close-up showing the card sash-window frames with scribed brick lintels above. The panelled front door was again made up from layers of card.

The model pub now bears its name and a painted panel with the name of the brewery.

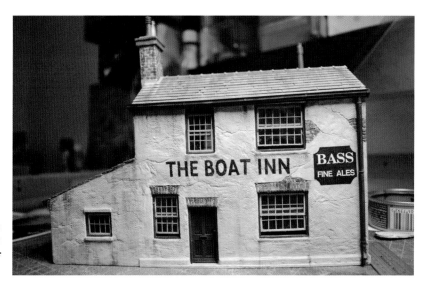

The two-storey canal-side pub on which this model was based used to stand in Burton upon Trent and was finished with render. No More Cracks plaster was used to achieve this effect.

The slates for the pub's roof were cut from card. This view illustrates the brickwork scribed for the gable parapet and the chimney stack, and gives a good indication of the weathering applied to finish the model.

Card was again used for the front bay window frames in this larger scale model, with the curtains made from tissue paper.

scratched with a scalpel in the same way. The strips of printed colour can then be spray mounted onto the facade of the building. This method can also be used on the facade of any other buildings with tiled decoration, such as cinemas, hotels and tube stations. The pub's name, and in most cases that of the brewery, will also need to be incorporated into the facade. Some corner pubs have the door situated on the actual corner, set at an angle of forty-five degrees to the corner wall. The pub and brewery names were placed on the panel above the doorway. The general principles will be the same for models of town centre and city public houses, although the buildings will be much larger.

Large hotels require a lot more work, especially if the facade incorporates classical decoration. Follow the suggestions you will find in the discussion of how to make a model of a Regency town house (*see* Chapter 2). Other details that will have to be added include the hotel name, curtains behind the deep sash windows, a foyer entrance and perhaps a flagpole.

SHOPS AND COMMERCIAL BUSINESSES

The high street would not be complete without an array of shops and commercial businesses along its length or, at the other extreme, the corner shop

A typical iron merchant's shop front at Blists Hill Victorian Town.

A PROJECT TO CONSTRUCT A GROCERY SHOP FRONT

Over the next few pages I will show how a convincing grocery shop front can be constructed in 7mm scale. The techniques and materials used can be adopted to any other shop trader along the high street, or to the common corner shop. Although this model has been constructed in 7mm scale the techniques and materials can be used for some of the smaller model railway scales.

On a visit to a doll's house supplier's show room, my eye was taken by the wooden mouldings sold as accessories such as skirting boards and picture rails for the 1/12th scale doll's houses. After close inspection I realised that these could be adapted for 7mm shop façades. The mouldings in question are supplied by The Doll's House Emporium.

Another accessory in the range was these chamfered panels

intended to make up corner quoins in the doll's houses. However, I could see a use for them on the 7mm shop fronts.

A selection of the mouldings and panels purchased from The Doll's House Emporium.

Putting the skirting board together with the picture rail moulding would give a good representation of the type and style of shop facia I was looking for.

The skirting board moulding would also make a reasonable plinth wall for buildings in both 7mm and 4mm scales.

Using the mouldings and cut-down chamfered panels together with fluted styrene sheet, I had the components to make up a reasonable shop front.

The components starting to come together.

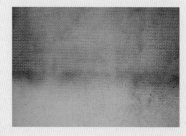

The walls for the shop were faced with styrene embossed brick sheet. This was first painted with a light coat of Halfords red oxide primer spray paint.

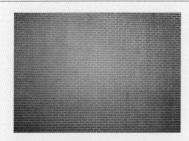

The next stage was to create the mortar colour and then to dry brush the brick shades over the face of the embossed brick work using oil paint. Chapter 5 includes a detailed account of these processes.

The shop façade has been assembled together and spray painted with a matt grass green colour produced by Humbrol. I created the lettering on the facia on my computer using the Copperplate font, which seemed to suit my requirements.

If you have a steady hand you could try painting the lettering onto the facia. I drew and spaced out the lettering first, before painting the

letter forms in white designers gouache paint, with a 00 brush. The letter forms were then given a drop shadow using a black fine liner pen.

In this photograph the shop front has moved on substantially. The façade complete with the pillars and facia board has been fitted into the front wall of the building. The front window framing and glazing has been added, together with framing over the door. The low support wall for the front window has also been added. This and the window framing were all constructed from card of different thicknesses.

The next job was to give the window support walls a coating of

the ready-mixed plaster to achieve a rendered finish.

Now I could turn my attention to the shop window display. I needed a grassy matt, of the kind that you often see in a greengrocers, for the display to stand on. I found that a small piece of surgical lint spray-painted grass green created just what I was looking for in 7mm scale.

In this picture the baskets and wooden trays of fruit and vegetables have been put out on display in the window. The door and door frame has also been fitted again using varying thicknesses of card sheet.

The fruit and vegetables have been placed on display outside the front of the shop. All the baskets and the wooden trays used were from the Skytrex 7mm range, with only the painting required to finish them.

A finishing touch was to add the price offers onto the window, which were painted onto the glass using white wash paint on the prototype. This was replicated by hand painting them onto the models glazing using white designer's gouache.

Another view looking down on the shop keeper's produce arranged in front of the shop.

The next job was to apply the lead flashings where the wooden shop façade meets the brick wall. This was achieved in miniature by using a strip of foil that I burnished around the joins to make a convincing replication of the real thing.

The final finishing touch to the model was to add a few enamelled advertising signs. These particular samples came from N Brass.

The facade of the chemist's shop, also at Blists Hill Victorian Town.

The facade of this grocer's shop has an unusual bowed top with added gable. Note the ornate finials and the highly decorative cornice.

at end of the terrace. Shops come in all shapes and sizes, from department stores downwards. The main purpose of a shop front is to display its produce as appealingly as possible in order to entice the public inside to make a purchase. The building above the shop will reflect the architecture of when it was built, but the shop facade itself can change with fashion. The early styles would normally consist of two large bay windows with multiple panes. The bays could be either square or curved.

The entrance to the shop would be placed between the two windows, within which displays were often arranged on shelves. From the Victorian era the shop windows would have larger panes arranged in double, triple or even more panelled frames. The tall glazed panels might be finished with a curved top to the frame. This type of frame could be in the form of a bay or just flat faced. The door might still be positioned in the centre or moved to one side. The top fascia would accommodate the shop's

Note the produce displayed in the draper's shop window, as well as the curved cornice and fascia board.

name and a box to contain a roller blind, which could be rolled out as protection from both rain and sunlight. Carved and fluted side columns were also used to frame the whole facade. During the Art Deco period modern lines were adopted by shops and especially the department stores. This period also saw the introduction of large glazed picture frames that were to become the norm, at least in towns and city centres.

MODELLING SHOPS

The buildings that accommodate shops can be of any style, period or size. I will therefore concentrate on how to create the shop facade in model form rather than the whole shop building.

Victorian shop fronts, including the name board panel, can be fabricated from layers of card or Plastikard, although I would recommend having the more ornate frames etched or laser cut. It might also be worthwhile having the fascia panels and

The butcher's shop at Blists Hill, with its two display bay windows, presents a plainer frontage than some examples. The advertising sign painted on the gable end wall is worth noting.

A large corner shop in Belper illustrates how the shop facade is an extension of the building's decorative architectural features. The fascia and cornice extends around the octagonal turret on the facing corner. This view also shows the weathering on the roof where the lead flashing has stained the slates.

This large shop from Ogmore Vale, rebuilt at St Fagans National History Museum, was both a general stores and an ironmonger's. It has extended display windows and two entrance doors to give access to both parts of the business.

This Edwardian draper's shop in Belper has been converted into living accommodation.

A row of shops in Burton upon Trent incorporating two corner units at each end of the block. Note the decorative parapet to the top of the row, with a gable positioned in the centre.

This view looking above the shop fronts of the Coronation Building in Burton shows its the modern lines. The rectangular metal-framed windows used here echo Art Deco designs.

supporting columns etched or laser cut. You will have to construct an appropriate inside display, as this will be visible through the large glazed windows. Use card to make a box with angled shelves, to which can be fixed a display of whatever produce is to be sold. The name board panel will require hand lettering, although sheets of pre-printed self-adhesive signs are available from companies such as Tiny Signs. For something more individual you might use dry-transfer lettering or create the lettering with computer software. You could also try photo-graphing shop signs using a digital camera. Britain's living museums have numerous samples of original

shop fronts, including the fascia boards with original signwriting. You can convert images of these to the scale required using Photoshop or a similar graphics package. The printed photograph can then be cut out and fixed to your model. One thing to remember when cutting out and pasting a printed image is that the white edge to the paper will be visible. This can be masked by running around the edge with a fine felt tip pen matching the colour of the background. You can also use the photographic method to produce advertising or point of sale signs inside the shop and around the window display. These little extras can also be had from Tiny Signs.

Corner pillar head of a shop front.

Modern fluting used on the door and window casements of a shop's corner entrance.

Another corner pillar, showing the decorative cornice supported on ornately carved corbels.

The pillar head is here topped with a small gable and supported on fluted brackets.

A very ornate pillar head with decorative carving and a sphere to top the finial.

The decorative frame seen in conjunction with the panelling and ornate cornice.

Another gable-topped pillar head supported on a carved bracket or corbel. There is a jetted cornice and the lead cap was intended to protect the gable from the weather.

Detailed view of the decorative framing at the top of the window frame.

The detail to the pillar, corbel and spherical top finial are all shown again, but now they have been moulded and cast in terracotta.

KITS AND OFF-THE-SHELF MODELS

Bilt-eezi, Superquick, Howard Scenics and Metcalfe all produce models of the corner terrace shop, usually as an add-on to the standard terrace house kit. Superquick also makes a row of shops in low relief. There is a plastic kit for a shop in the Airfix range now sold under the name of Dapol.

Bachmann's Scenecraft range includes quite a few ready-made models, although the corner shop is the only one modelled in full. The others are modelled in low relief and include a corner café, fish and chip shop, launderette and newsagent.

The shops in Hornby's Skaledale range that are modelled in full include a city dry-cleaner's, antiques shop, record store, pet shop, florist, television and radio shop, hardware store and sports shop.

COMMERCIAL AND PUBLIC SERVICE BUILDINGS

For the last part of this chapter I will look at some of the many commercial and public service buildings that have been at the heart of towns and cities and often dominated them. Town halls, from where local and sometimes county council business is conducted, have always been provided with an imposing building. Whether the architecture is Georgian, Regency, Victorian or Art Deco in style, decorative embellishments would be employed to emphasize the building's importance and status. One form of decoration that frequently appears is the display in a

Burton upon Trent Town Hall, in the Gothic Revival style, has an impressive clock tower and buttresses topped with sculpted lions. Also note the stone corner quoins and cornice work.

The elaborate Market Town House in the Market Place at Abingdon, Oxfordshire. Note the steep hipped roof complete with dormers.

The west elevation of Burton upon Trent Town Hall, showing the Gothic arches and the round stained-glass window provided in the gable. Note the elaborate cornice positioned above the arches.

The Municipal Offices, built next to the Town Hall in the 1930s, reflects the Art Deco style of that period.

The Portland stone central projection uses set-back fluting to create a casement surround to the central windows and the door. Note the civic arms carved above the main door.

prominent position of the civic coat of arms. Town halls were often equipped with clock towers, turrets and domes, while a Palladian frontage might have balconies from which the mayor and other dignitaries would address their audiences.

Other public buildings closely associated with the town halls might include a museum, art gallery and public library. These were often similarly grand and decorative, built in the fashionable classical or Gothic Revival styles. Depending on the style chosen, these

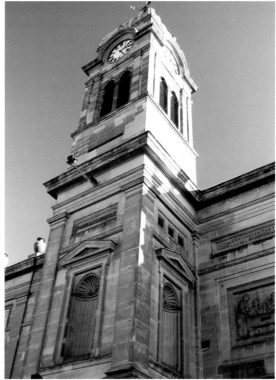

The Central Library, Museum and Art Gallery in Derby displays impressive Gothic embellishments in both brick and stone, and is crowned with a magnificent clock tower.

The stone facade and clock tower of Derby's Guild Hall stands proudly over the Market Place.

BELOW: *This Portland stone arch is the entrance to the Abbey Arcade in Burton. Note the use of a classical Greek frieze above the elaborate keystoned arch.*

RIGHT: *The design of the Magistrates Court in Burton, incorporating classical Greek pillars, decorative cornices and elaborate parapets surrounding a dome, reflects the building's importance in the town. This was also built using Portland stone.*

The choice of Tuscan columns for the Portland stone surround of a museum's main entrance is designed to emphasize the archaic.

The impressive building of Ellis of Burton has an octagonal corner tower with a bell-shaped top clad with copper. The building is finished with red brick and gritstone details.

buildings might also incorporate clock towers or domes.

Public buildings were also needed for the imposition of law and order. Law courts, for example, would be housed in grand classical buildings designed to evoke power and authority. Police stations, too, were meant to reflect their importance in serving the community. Also serving the law were solicitors, whose offices might be found in large town houses or modern office blocks.

Buildings were also required to serve the health of the local community. Doctors and dentists often established their surgeries in the grand town houses. Hospitals have always been large buildings in the prevailing architectural style, right up to the ultra-modern super-hospitals of today, although these are

now generally built on the outskirts of an urban area rather than at its centre.

Ambulance and fire stations served the emergency services. These facilities were often located in the suburbs rather than in the town centre. There would be extensive garage space for the emergency vehicles, together with accommodation and facilities to meet the recreational requirements of the staff. Fire stations would also include a tower to provide practice when replicating fighting fires in multi-storey buildings.

Moving back to the high street, the room space above the shops would be occupied by commercial and public businesses, such as insurance companies and estate agents. Such businesses were also to be found in purpose-built offices of all sizes and styles,

Another brick building with stone casements, cornices and pillars supporting a dome.

The rotunda tower of the former Northcliffe House in Derby has an impressive copper-clad cupola, topped with a large ball finial, which is visible on the skyline from many parts of the city.

The Oakdale Workmen's Institute, which has been rebuilt at St Fagans National History Museum, included a purpose-built library and reading rooms, a concert hall across the whole first floor and recreational rooms. Note the balcony under the central gable.

This building displays simpler lines but still has a simplified cornice and casements to the windows and doors. The white stucco finish stands out against the ultramarine sky.

The offices of the former Derby and Derbyshire Banking Company were intended to demonstrate the company's financial importance. Note the intricate roofline cornice and the carved coat of arms on the pediment.

In complete contrast, this concrete and glass office block from the 1970s houses insurance and finance companies.

This corner building houses financial offices above the shop units. The Gothic Revival elements in the design were common in the Victorian era.

The impressive corner tower of the Midland Railway Institute, topped by a copper-clad conical cupola, complete with a flag pole.

The Midland Railway Institute was built by the company to meet the workers' educational and recreational requirements. The building had both reading and games rooms, with a large concert hall and lounges.

The Midland Hotel in Derby, built close to the station, was one of the first railway hotels. Competition between the railway companies was intense and no expense was spared to demonstrate the company's wealth and importance.

including the steel and smoked-glass blocks that tower over the urban skyline today.

Banks and building societies also attempted to create an impression of power and security on the high street by opting for classical architectural styles, although in recent years the changing nature of their operations has led to much of their business being conducted in high-rise glass towers.

The transport services always required their own distinctive buildings. The rival railway companies employed the best architects to design and build stations and their associated hotels to symbolize the company's power (see above). Tram systems, which offered clean and efficient transportation within the urban centres, were mostly owned and run by the town and city councils and corporations. The tram lines were later extended into the suburbs to provide a service to and from town. Sheds were required to store and maintain the trams and large depots were built by the town council or private companies. The trams disappeared from the streets in the post-war years as they tended to clog up the streets and were deemed to be old-fashioned as they could only go where the tracks and overhead power lines were installed. Trolleybuses were a transitional means of transport as they used the overhead electric power supply but were more flexible as they did not require rails. These again would need depots, although most probably occupied the old tram sheds. Buses would eventually be the favoured public transport system, with bus garages being required as well as the bus

station. The local routes would not only link the centres with the suburbs, but would also provide services to neighbouring towns and surrounding villages, creating a service to passengers into the town. Since the early 1990s tram and light rail services have returned to the streets and suburbs of some of our major cities.

MODELLING COMMERCIAL AND PUBLIC BUILDINGS

In order to make models from scratch of the various civic buildings mentioned above, you should make use of the construction methods described earlier but make allowance for some complicated additions. For example, in order to make numbers of ornate door and window cases, decorative pillars, cornices, corbels and facing decoration you will need to create a master of each architectural element. This can then be used to make a silicone mould from which the components can be cast in resin or plaster. Some parts, such as balconies and parapet decoration, might be better etched or laser-cut, depending on their intricacy and how many you require. The other buildings will be easier to build from scratch.

If you are modelling a modern layout and wish to include an office block, my advice would be to consider building a clear box, using the thicker clear sheets available from Evergreen as this will make the box more stable. Use a clear polystyrene cement to bond the joints, trying to achieve as clean a joint as possible.

A decorative parapet with open balustrade tops this small facade in Burton.

The stone lintels of the Exchange Buildings in Derby are of interest.

RIGHT: *The National Westminster Bank occupies this Art Deco building in Derby. Note the design's use of right angles, for example on the square clock.*

The framework to the building can be cut by hand, but if you require large areas to be covered I would advise drawing it first and then having this laser-cut.

A few kits of smaller civic buildings are available in card from Superquick, Metcalfe and other suppliers. There are a police station and a market house, for example, in the Superquick range. Both Superquick and Metcalfe supply a bank and building society in low relief combined with a row of shops (the Metcalfe example being three storeys high). The same two companies also produce a large station frontage and a tram or bus depot kit.

Off-the-shelf examples from Bachmann's Scenecraft range include a small office block and an ambulance station. There is also a solicitor's business in a period town house modelled in low relief.

You may encounter other models and kits, but the samples I have suggested should give you a rea-sonable start in replicating a typical urban street scene. If you are looking for something less typical and more closely based on a certain town, you can always turn to building from scratch. This will take more time and effort, but the rewards will certainly be more satisfying, giving you a model of which you can be proud.

RIGHT: *The ultra-modern glass and steel atrium of a new hotel in Derby is an example of the architecture that would fit into a contemporary urban scene if you are modelling the railways of today.*

THE CREATION OF AN EDWARDIAN STREET SCENE

This section shows how an Edwardian street scene has been modelled to perfection. The street fronts the scale seven model 'Dewsbury Goods', which is now being completed by members of the Historical Model Railway Society. The HMRS has its headquarters and study centre linked to the Mathew Kirtley museum, which is part of The Midland Railway Centre at Swanwick, near Ripley, Derbyshire. The building is open to the public on certain days and weekends of the year. Check out the HMRS website for further details of open days and membership.

The buildings featured in the following photographs were all constructed in kit form by Chris Perry in New Zealand, before being shipped over to the UK where members of the HMRS then assembled the buildings and located them into their final position.

The cobbled street fronting the shops was laid down using cast resin panels that had been reproduced from a master scribed out in Das modelling clay. To complete the scene the model has been dressed with figures, all in Edwardian costume, horse-drawn commercial drays, a pillar box and numerous advertising signs.

The shipping agent's office, which is located close to the railway goods yard. The walls and window displays are all adorned with signs that advertise the great variety of goods the agent is able to ship, ranging from coal to small parcels. All these signs have been hand-painted using a 00 brush.

The double frontage of the town pub, advertising the ales, stout, and porter available for consumption inside.

A close-up of the shipping agent's office, with a couple interested in one of the services available. Note also the flower seller trying to sell her wares on the street corner. It is little touches like this that bring our models to life.

Here another delightful cameo has been modelled, with a lady and gentleman in deep conversation. The figures are from the S&D Models range, and have been hand painted by Paul Clarke.

The newsagent & tobacconist's shop, Just look at the detail that has been added to the shop window display, again all executed by hand.

Another photograph of B. Miller's, shop showing more advertising signs added to the walls. Note also the net curtains to the windows; this shows the modeller's keen eye for detail.

A different view of the pub, with the centre signage displaying the pub's name, The Brunswick Arms.

Another dressing to complete the street scene is the horse-drawn dray – a very common sight for the period in which the model has been placed. This particular vehicle, a dray belonging to The London & North Western and Great Northern Joint Railway, was modelled by Nelson Twells, and was donated to the HMRS by Bob Essery.

This wider view of the shop fronts reveals an entry to a back yard business of Perry Bros Builders.

This is a lovely cameo, showing the postman in conversation with Mrs Goodhall, the shop proprietor. Again note the attention for detail shown in the shop signage and the elaborate window display.

CHAPTER FOUR

CREATING THE URBAN SETTING

So far I have tried to cover the diverse variety of urban buildings that you may choose to include on a model railway. In this chapter I will turn to how these can be placed into a convincing urban setting, starting with the infrastructure that supports domestic houses as well as the commercial and public buildings found on the high street. The second part will take a look at urban dereliction and decay, examining how this might be portrayed. I will conclude with an exercise to show how perspective can be exploited to achieve greater depth and realism.

STREET SCENES

Nearly all the houses in an urban area will be built on or close to a street, under which or running alongside there will be all the services required for the properties: gas, electricity, telephone, water and sewage.

In towns and cities the road surface was a covering of cobbles or granite setts; the latter was favoured, owing to its hard-wearing properties. The replacement of this with tarmac asphalt, even though

A scrapyard next to the railway. Adding features such as this to a model railway provides extra detail to an urban landscape. Photo: Andy Peters

The streets of many British towns were covered with granite setts.

Tram lines were set within the granite setts. This example also shows the plate over the tie rod connecting a point at the Crich Tramway Museum in Derbyshire.

Note the York kerbstones in this view of the gutter between a cobbled street and a flagstone pavement.

Different materials are used here for the pavement and the kerbs. The pavement consists of blue Victorian paving setts and the kerb is made from iron edging panels. This was common in industrial areas such as the Black Country.

This pavement consists of Victorian terracotta setts, while the kerb is of blue-black bull-nosed bricks. Also seen here is an iron drain cover in position along the gutter.

The Yorkstone flags covering this pavement were commonly found in many towns and cities. It is always worth adding such details as the cracked flag to your models.

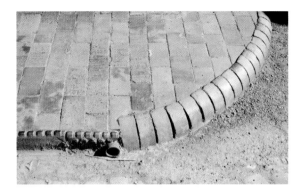

A mix of materials on a pavement's corner section. The covering is made up of blue paving blocks, with bull-nosed blocks forming the kerb and iron plates on the straight section. Note the use of asphalt and cobbles for the road surface at the junction.

Asphalt is the most commonly used road surface.

it is not as hard-wearing, was well advanced by the 1950s. Cobbles, however, can still be found in some back streets and industrial yards.

Along each side of the road would be pavements giving pedestrian access. The pavement consisted of a raised, hard-surfaced pathway with a top covering of cobbles, granite setts, stone flags or blue brick pavers. Sometimes a mixture of these materials was used. The later preference was for a covering of concrete slabs or tarmac, but recently brick pavers have been used again. The pavement was raised to create a gutter for rainwater to run off the surface of the road and away into a drain. The step in between was edged with a row of kerbstones or sometimes there was an iron edging strip, especially where brick pavers were used. The gutter was sometimes lined with granite setts even though the road surface was asphalt. Cast iron drain covers would be positioned along the gutter at regular intervals.

MODELLING THE STREETS

A cobbled surface or granite setts can be made by applying a thin layer of Das modelling clay into a coating of PVA. When the clay has completely dried the cobbles can then be scribed out. I would recommend scribing for those occasions when you are trying to replicate cobbles of irregular sizes. If the sets are regular, then you can use a pre-scribed sheet

of cobbles. Those available from Wills are very good for this, but you will need to splice them together. Try using a plaster filler or a little Das to fill the gap and mask the join. You can even scribe into the clay, continuing the cobbles. Alternative methods are to use embossed card or polystyrene sheets. I have used the sheets from Metcalfe on my own layout 'Tawcombe'. As with the Wills sheets, care will be needed when joining the sheets together. The advantage of using embossed polystyrene sheets is that the sheet size is much larger and so a bigger area may be covered without too many joins. For the 7mm modeller Skytrex produces panels of pre-scribed irregular cobbles cast in resin, as well as extra joining panels that combine to form a T-junction. Let-in strips are also available so that tram lines can be added to the Skytrex streets.

Roads with an asphalt finish can be modelled in various ways. For a rough finish try using No More Cracks plaster filler, which gives a convincing texture when brushed into PVA. Another way of achieving the finish is to sieve fine ballast into PVA. This effect can look better on the larger scale models, but it really depends on how fine the ballast is in the first place. Texture spray paints are available at most DIY stores and can create a good replication of an asphalted road. To create re-tarmacked roads, try using sheets of wet and dry paper, which can be easily cut to size and glued down with PVA. There will be joins to deal with but they will not be noticed if the sheets are fitted well.

PARTS AND ACCESSORIES FOR COMMERCIAL BUILDINGS AND STREET SCENES

This section shows a few accessories and parts that might help you with the finishing touches required for your commercial buildings, or add to both the street and back yard scenes to complement your buildings. I have deliberately included some modern items as well as those from the past to give you a better choice and understanding of what is available on the market. Adding the finishing touches and set dressings, if done properly, will bring your models to life and give that little extra touch of realism to any model railway.

These laser-cut brackets are available from York Model Making. They can be used to support a hoist house or as support brackets for a canopy on a shopping arcade.

4mm brackets in the form of brass etchings available from the Scale-Link range. These more ornate samples would make excellent support brackets for a Victorian arcade or canopy fronting a row of shops.

A set of doors complete with an arched light over the top. These would complement any commercial building such as a bank. These laser-cut samples in card are available from Truetexture.

Laser-cut valancing, available from York Model Making. Although this is mainly intended for railway station canopies, there is no reason why it can't be used to dress the canopies of a shopping arcade or market stall.

Trays and boxes of fresh fish, available as white metal castings from Skytrex Models. These are ideal to dress the counters and displays of a fishmonger's shop or market stall. They can also be used on a fish dock or on a model of a quayside, where they have perhaps just been unloaded from a fishing boat.

These white metal packing cases produced by Skytrex Models would be useful items to dress any commercial loading bay of a back street business.

Like the packing cases, these white metal pallets from the Skytrex 7mm range would not look out of place on a loading bay or builder's yard.

A very useful item to dress a street on a modern image layout is this loaded refuse skip. This particular one is produced in resin from the 7mm Skytrex range, and even comes complete with an old mattress.

Skytrex have now produced a tall round chimney in 4mm scale. It would be ideal for any mill, factory, colliery or a brewery model. It comes with optional square flue base. The author was responsible for creating the masters where every brick, like the bottle oven was scribed out by hand.

For the modern-image modeller, these metal chemical containers from Skytrex would suit a commercial loading bay or industrial yard.

A curved hooded ventilator from Skytrex in 4mm scale. These can used to finish the roof of a factory or bus depot.

A selection of baskets containing fresh fruit and vegetables, to dress the inside and outside of a grocers shop or market stall. These are available from the Skytrex Models 7mm range of accessories. I have used these to full effect on the grocer's shop front project.

Different sizes of wooden barrels or casks, ideal for any brewery or being delivered to the local High Street public house. Also you might see them stored in the back yard of any hostelry. These are available in 7mm from Skytrex and Duncan Models.

This section shows how to model granite setts. The cobbles and the pavement are scribed into a skin of Das modelling clay, which is then applied to a card base. Thicker card is used for the pavement base, with the kerbstones scribed to the edge.

For this combination of cobbles and asphalt, the cobbles are scribed into the Das modelling clay and the surface of the asphalt is fabricated using fine ballast.

The finished and painted granite setts. The compo is applied using the residue powder created during the scribing process. This is brushed into the scribed gaps and then fixed using a matt fixative spray.

On this demonstration panel the asphalt surface on the left has been created using textured spray paint. The right side was made from a coat of No More Cracks plaster filler, applied into a pre-coat of PVA using a stipple action with the brush. This method gives better results for finer asphalted roads.

Stone-textured spray paint gives a good representation of the rougher asphalt road surface.

A selection of materials to replicate asphalted roads: (left) fine white ballast; (centre) finer ballast, available in a natural grey colour, gives a good replication without the need for painting.

The result of spray painting to a rougher surface, using Humbrol Matt Tank Grey.

Humbrol Matt Tank Grey, now available in a spray, gives a convincing colour finish for an asphalted road surface.

The demonstration panel showing the effect when spray painted using Humbrol Matt Tank Grey. Both surfaces give a good representation of the asphalted prototypes.

These panels with granite setts and a paved pavement section are available in resin in 7mm scale from Skytrex Models.

The yard next to the Vegetable Warehouse. Note the detail of the gates, gaslights and cobbles, all modelled by Martin Nield for his pre-grouping layout 'Eccleston'.

The raised pavement will require a sub-base. For a 4mm scale model use mounting board, which, at about 2–3mm thick, would represent a kerb rise of 6 to 9 inches. Thicker card will have to be selected for 7mm models, such as Corri-Core board, which is available from most picture framers. A thin skin of Das modelling clay can be added to this. Cobbles or stone flags can be scribed onto the surface when dry. The kerbstones will also need to be scribed into the clay on the facing edge. For asphalt-surfaced pavements, this can be replicated by brushing No More Cracks plaster filler into a thin coating of PVA. Textured spray paint could also be used, but the kerbstones will still need to be added.

In 7mm scale Skytrex has produced resin pavement strips and corner quadrant pieces that fit the cobbled street panels. For the 4mm scale modeller, there are embossed card alternatives from companies such as Metcalfe.

In order to put a finishing touch to gutters, drain covers should be fixed in place; these are available as brass etchings from firms, including Scalelink. Grates provided for deliveries to coal cellars are to be found on pavements right up against the front wall of each house. These became redundant with the introduction of central heating and most have been covered over.

STREET LIGHTING

One service that was definitely provided in towns was street lighting. The first systems for providing light relied on gas. Some back streets were still fitted with gas lighting up to the 1960s, using coal gas supplied from the local gasworks. By then, however, electricity had become the choice to power every street lighting requirement. Also in the 1960s sodium lighting was introduced. It gave more light but at the expense of more light spread. In recent years, however, a start has been made on replacing sodium lights with systems that produce a more efficient and brighter white light than was available previously.

Models of various types of street lights are available. While most are just cosmetic, working lights have

Until the 1950s many urban streets were still lit by gaslight.

Some examples of the early Victorian design of hexagonal pillar box with an ornate cap are still in use.

become popular in recent years now that microelectronics has given model-makers the choice of adding scale lighting to model railways. Try looking at the ranges produced by Kytes Lights, RMLectronics and DCCconcepts of Australia, the last of whom offers both gas and swan-neck lamps that are ideal for a British street scene.

STREET FURNITURE

Street scenes would not be complete without the items of street furniture with which we are all familiar. Most of these, such as red pillar boxes, telephone boxes and street signs, will be situated on the pavement. Pillar postboxes vary from ornamental octagonal Victorian designs to the more recent familiar round GPO boxes. Postboxes might also be built into walls, mounted on lamp posts or telegraph poles, or set on top of a metal or wooden post.

The later round pillar boxes are much more familiar. This type has a much simpler domed cap.

The familiar red telephone box design may still be found in conservation areas.

Pillar boxes are often seen mounted into a wall.

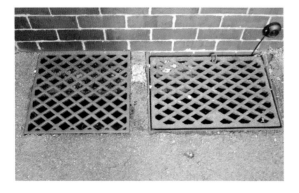

Terraced rows often have coal cellar grilles, used to deliver the fuel, positioned on the pavement.

A coal cellar grille like this would be worth considering as an addition to a model.

The telephone box started to appear in the mid-1920s to a design by Sir Giles Gilbert Scott that changed little through to the Jubilee Kiosk of 1935, known as the K6. In 1959 Neville Conder was commissioned by the GPO to modernize the box. The resulting K7 had much cleaner lines but it did not enter production. Bruce Martin's K8 design, however, which employed single panels of glass in all three glazed sides, was manufactured from 1968 to 1983. Under British Telecom the KX100 kiosk was introduced from 1984. This was a much more utilitarian design that began to replace most of the traditional boxes, although a few red boxes still remain in conservation areas. With massive owner-ship of the personal mobile phone, however, there is now little demand for public phone boxes and this piece of street furniture is now almost extinct.

STREET SIGNS

Street name signs were usually cast with raised black letters on a white plate background that, especially in

Cast street name signs with scalloped corners.

Cast sign on a Regency terrace in Derby.

A later enamelled street name sign.

Two cast street name signs arranged on a corner.

Glazed tiles provide a decorative surround on a butcher's shop.

Enamelled advertising signs were often placed on urban buildings.

The gable end of a terrace offers a prominent advertising site for another butcher.

Any space in the view of the general public, such as these enamelled advertising signs fixed to a fence, might be used to display advertising.

An advertising 'V' board for Hovis bread. This style of board is now more commonly used by estate agents and property developers.

Enamelled advertising signs are available on the model railway market from Tiny Signs.

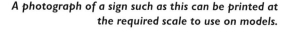

A photograph of a sign such as this can be printed at the required scale to use on models.

the Victorian period, might have a fancy border. Later signs were enamelled, with white letters produced flat on a dark blue background. The signs were either mounted on the front walls of buildings or on posts positioned along the pavement. Beside the street names, road signs were also placed on the streets to give orders, warnings and advice to the road user.

Street advertising was very common in the late Victorian and Edwardian periods, when a mass of advertising boards and enamelled signs decorated the streets. Advertising hoardings were positioned wherever there was space. Any spare gable end of a terrace would be festooned with hoardings. Such hoardings are still in common use today, although the advertisements pasted on them have changed somewhat. If you are creating a modern layout you may wish to include the bright neon signs that appear in the centre of larger towns and cities.

There are other items of street furniture you may wish to include, such as telegraph poles, bollards, dustbins, benches and litter bins.

MODELLING STREET FURNITURE

Small items to complete dressing a street scene can be had from Dart Castings, Langley Models, Shire Scenes and Springside Models for 4mm scale and smaller, and from S&D Models for 7mm scale. For signs and posters, the ranges supplied by Tiny Signs cover most model railway scales. Hoardings can be constructed from styrene using sheet material and strip for the framework.

There are a few suppliers of street furniture, with ranges covering most of the scales. Hornby's Skaledale range supplies both traditional red and modern-style telephone boxes, as well as a police box. Langley and Springside Models produce a traditional box in

A more modern scene is depicted in this photograph. A Class 33 diesel trundles across the elevated brick viaducts, taking a train across a superbly modelled London urban landscape. The 'Stoney Lane Depot' layout is the work of Grahame Hedges.

Small businesses and lock-ups can often be found within the back streets.

accessories may not be complete, so I would advise that you browse the internet or check displays on exhibition stands, where companies may introduce newly released items.

AROUND THE BACK

So far I have only discussed the fronts of houses and other buildings along the street. We can now take a look around the backs. Terraces would often have a back entry and passage, known in some parts of the North of England as the ginnel. The passages would usually have a surface made up of cobbles or paver bricks; later these might have been resurfaced with asphalt. Each side of the passageway would be walled or fenced to the backyards of the properties. Until the 1960s behind each house there would be an outhouse to contain the outside toilet and coalhouses. Sometimes there might also be a wash house at the back of the yard. Coal would be delivered down the passageway to the coal houses. The original toilets would have to been emptied by night soil men, employed by the local authority. The other item to be emptied regularly was domestic rubbish, so dustbins would also be put out along these passages on the day of collection. The terraced rows often backed on to the railway line. As you approach any large town or city by train, you will most certainly pass the backs of housing stock like this. In the railway towns most of the terraces would have housed railway workers and it was common for the perimeter fence between the railway and the properties to be made from old sleepers, a detail that would be worth adding to your urban model railway.

Many small businesses, such as builders' and stonemasons' yards, were set up in and around the backyards, behind the entries and along the labyrinths of passageways. There were also garages and lock-ups. These businesses could be found occupying the space underneath any railway arch and this would make an interesting feature, running your trains above the streets below. I will cover this concept in greater detail later.

white metal. Hornby also supplies red pillar and wall-mounted postboxes, while Langley, Shire Scenes and Springside produces the same types, but as unpainted white-metal models. The Hornby Skaledale range includes dustbins, wheelie bins, skips and litter bins, as well as benches, crossing beacons, road signs and a bus shelter. Most of these are also available in white metal from the likes of Langley, Shire Scenes and Springside, and in resin from Ten Commandments for 4mm scale and Skytrex for 7mm scale. This list of

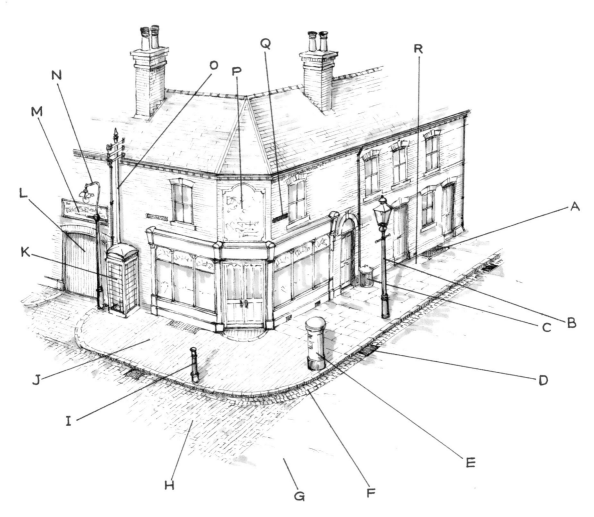

Street corner scene with a typical Victorian terrace, illustrating the street furniture that can be added to dress a model: (A) coal cellar grilles; (B) gas lamp standard; (C) galvanized dustbin; (D) cast iron grate cover; (E) round pillar box; (F) cobbled gutter; (G) asphalted road surface; (H) cobbled granite setts; (I) cast iron bollard; (J) blue-black paving blocks; (K) standard (K6) telephone box; (L) doors and entry to a backyard business; (M) advertising sign for the small business; (N) electric lamp standard; (O) telegraph pole; (P) advertising panel painted on the corner wall; (Q) cast metal street name sign; (R) Yorkstone paving flags.

Garages were also a feature of the back-street terraces, as no provision for cars was needed when these houses were built.

Note the cobbled surface of the back passageway to a terrace row.

All terraced houses had the toilet, or privy, in the backyard.

Coalhouses were also to be found along the alleyways at the back of the houses.

Close-up of the outside water closet door showing the weathering detail.

These alleyway coalhouses have been built lower than normal.

Coalhouses are featured again in this back wall. Note the weathering to the stone of these hillside Yorkshire terraces and the cobbled alley in front.

Another backyard privy, showing how narrow
it would be, with just about enough room to
squeeze in.

Cobbled setts and centre rain gutter along a back
passageway in West Yorkshire. This covering might
be found all over the country.

This cast iron coal hatch
door, found in West
Yorkshire, was provided so
that coal could be delivered
directly into the back of
the coalhouse.

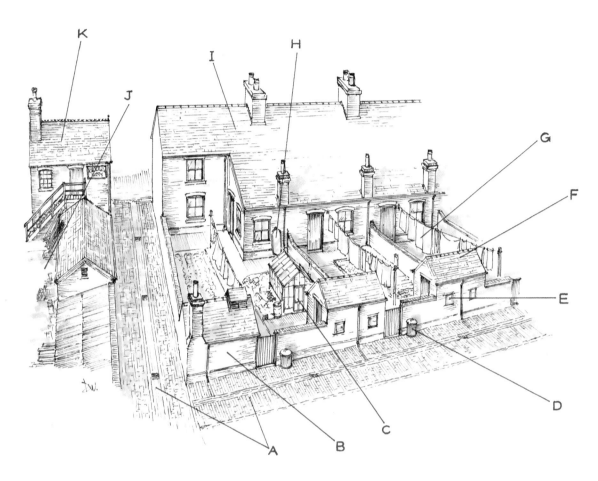

Features and items to be found at the back of a Victorian terrace row: (A) cobbled passage or alley with centre gutter, complete with cast drain covers; (B) backyard wash house; (C) greenhouse occupying the larger plot; (D) galvanized dustbins; (E) coal hatch; (F) combined coalhouse and outside privy; (G) washing lines running the length of the yards; (H) galvanized tin bath, stored in the yard until bath night; (I) terraced row; (J) builder's storage yard; (K) office to this back-street business.

Sign board displaying the light engineering trade of a back-street business.

The wash house was a common outbuilding to be found in the backyards. This sample has been rebuilt behind the terrace row at Blists Hill Victorian Town.

Yards for builders and stonemasons are often found in back streets or, as here, in alleyways. This example is also at Blists Hill Victorian Town.

Another small back-street business found in a purpose-built wooden shed.

ABOVE, LEFT: *On washday every terrace backyard would see the washing hung out to dry along the whole length of the short yard. This detail is worth adding as a finishing touch to any model.*

ABOVE, RIGHT: *A gateway through the wall of a terrace might give access to a backyard business.*

LEFT: *Backyards and alleys would not be complete without dustbins. White-metal models are available in most scales.*

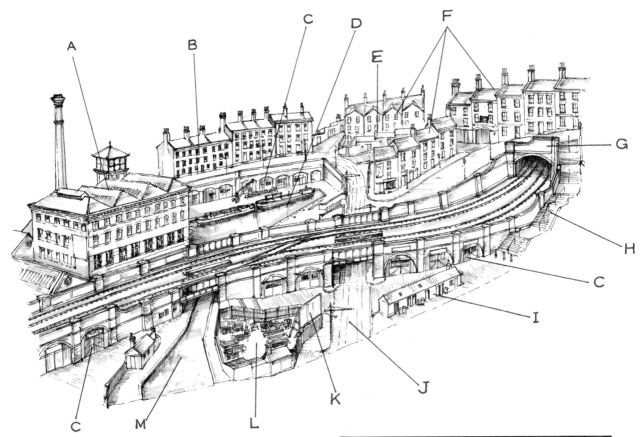

A Yorkshire mill town. The railway is in an elevated position, near the front of the model. Towards the far right the track disappears into a tunnel under the built-up urban landscape, as the buildings rise up the side of the valley: (A) large cotton textile mill; (B) rows of tenement houses, perhaps modelled in low relief and in a smaller scale; (C) lock-ups and small businesses established within the arches underneath; (D) canal basin; (E) outhouses for outside toilets and coal storage; (F) rows of terraced houses, built in a stepped arrangement as they climb the hillside; (G) brick-built tunnel mouth; (H) flights of steps to give pedestrian access to the higher town; (I) row of outhouses positioned across an alleyway; (J) cobbled street with tram lines set into the cobbles; (K) adveristing hoardings; (L) small builder's or stonemason's yard; (M) canal arm to serve the basin.

Early backyards would also have a water pump, such as this example at Blists Hill Victorian Town.

A row of outbuildings containing the privy and coalhouse, situated on the far side of the alleyway.

The same row of outbuildings, showing the door and chimney stack at the rear.

Cobbled backyard and outhouses in West Yorkshire.

Another row of outhouses backing on to an alleyway.

The back alleys and yards were often fenced with old railway sleepers, especially if they bordered railway property.

DERELICTION AND DECAY

The urban landscape has gone through a number of changes to its industry, housing and transport. Change brings with it the evidence of dereliction. When the old becomes redundant it takes a while before buildings are swept away or modernized.

The railways have provided many illustrations of this as the services were modernized or completely disposed of. The latter was certainly evident after the implementation of the Beeching report in the mid-1960s when thousands of miles of track were ripped up, making railway buildings redundant and left to decay. The railways had replaced the canals

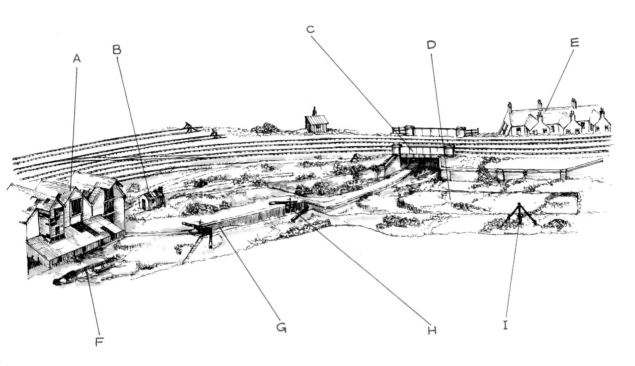

Urban dereliction as it might be modelled for a model railway depicting the 1950s or 1960s: (A) derelict canal warehouse, displaying broken windows and missing planks in the hoist house, together with slates and sheeting missing from the roofs; (B) charred remains of a wooden yard office after being set on fire. Note the lifted railway tracks where weeds and small bushes have begun to take over; (C) steel plate canal bridge; (D) reed-choked canal basin; (E) backs of terrace houses, showing the wooden buttresses to support the gable end of the row; (F) remains of a sunken narrow boat in the weed-choked basin; (G) lock chamber partly filled in with all sorts of rubbish; (H) broken lock gates still in position but slowly rotting away; (I) remains of a wooden derrick crane, from which the jib has long since been removed.

The weathering apparent on this derelict stone-built factory in Derbyshire is worth studying.

Detail of the same building showing the weathering stains created from the broken downpipe.

Note the broken windows on a derelict textile mill in West Yorkshire.

Derelict railway warehouse in Derby.

The remains of the lucam for loading goods up to the top floor.

Buddleia growing out of the masonry of a derelict mill in Belper, Derbyshire. This plant soon colonizes any derelict building and quickly established itself on urban bomb sites after the war.

Disused engine house supplied to work the floor lifts for the warehouse complex.

The broken windows of a disused factory is a feature worth including on a model of urban decay.

Now that the disused canal has been filled in, the stone bridge is left spanning nothing but earth.

for carrying the majority of goods, and these too began to be run down slowly from the early 1920s. Some were filled in but most were left as open tips, especially those in urban areas. If your model railway is set in the period from the 1930s through to the 1960s, a canal modelled in a derelict state with weed-choked channels and broken lock gates would not look out of place.

If your chosen period is during or just after the Second World War, it may be worth including bomb-damaged buildings on your layout. The mill towns of the north would change dramatically during

Different levels linked by steps can be used on a model as a means of saving space, while still giving an impression of depth to an urban scene. The background buildings on the highest level can be modelled at a smaller scale than those in the foreground.

the post-war period. Cotton mills started to close in the 1960s as they were unable to withstand cheaper imported textiles from the Far East, leaving these large imposing buildings to become derelict before final demolition. The mill chimneys were toppled one by one, changing the industrial landscape for ever. The buildings and structures of the other major industries would also become redundant, either by closure or by change. The familiar bottle ovens of Stoke-on-Trent's potteries were razed to the ground and replaced by gas-fired kilns. The collieries also disappeared one by one and by the early 1980s this major industry was more or less extinct in many regions. Modelling any of these industrial areas during this period would require portraying

A terrace row on a hillside. The stepped arrangement of the buildings can be modelled using perspective, with the furthest building being at a smaller scale than the nearest.

The different levels of terraced housing on a hillside. There is no reason why the terraced row in the background should not be modelled in a smaller scale.

industrial dereliction. Domestic housing also witnessed changes and modernization. There was a massive demolition programme as the streets of terraced housing were bulldozed in favour of high-rise blocks of flats. Rows of Victorian houses may still be seen boarded up awaiting their fate, even though we know that high-rise is definitely not the answer to the housing problem.

AN EXERCISE IN PERSPECTIVE MODELLING

Perspective can be used to great advantage when building an urban model railway. An illusion of distance and scale can be achieved in our models by careful planning and observation of the prototype. When carried out correctly this gives more depth to the model when viewed from the front and at the same time creates more space on the baseboard. This can be taken a stage further by using low relief

modelling for buildings positioned right at the back of the model.

This theory is explained in the accompanying diagrams. Here you can clearly see that any buildings modelled in the foreground and up to the railway will have to be modelled in that scale. If the railway is modelled in 4mm to 1ft scale (00 gauge), the buildings in front and in close proximity to the track will also need to be modelled in 4mm to 1ft scale. Any buildings positioned in the background away from the track, however, can be modelled at the smaller scale of 3mm or 2mm to 1ft (N gauge).

If a row of terraced buildings is included, with the gable end positioned facing the railway, then again this near gable must be modelled in the same scale. The gable at the far end of the terrace, however, can be modelled smaller with the walls and roof receding to that scale. Any walls and streets will also have to be modelled in the same way so that they recede together, giving the full effect of perspective.

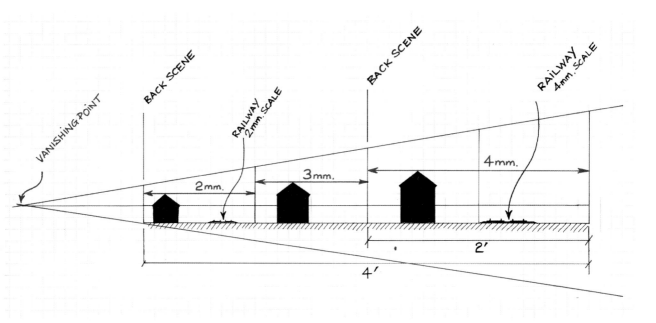

Scales can be mixed on an urban layout. Here a 4mm scale railway is accommodated in the foreground, while in the background a 2mm scale railway is employed. Plenty of depth is required if this effect is to be achieved: in this case there is about 1.2m from the front to the back.

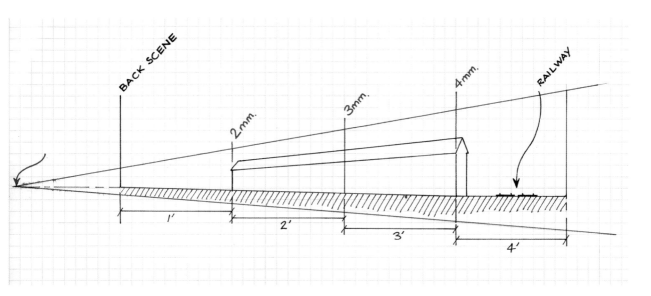

A terraced row of houses has here been positioned with the gable end at a right angle to the railway in the foreground. The row is modelled in 4mm scale at the near end, receding to 2mm scale at the far end. More can be accommodated in the space allocated on the baseboard by modelling in perspective. To give the full effect of perspective, however, the baseboard surface should be fixed at a shallow inclined angle.

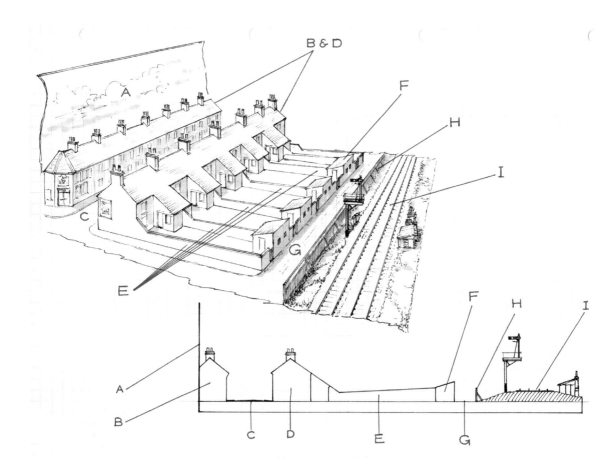

Using perspective and a mixture of scales together for terraced houses positioned parallel to the railway running in the foreground. The outhouses have been modelled to the same scale as the railway, but the terraced rows are to a smaller scale. To create the effect of perspective, the dividing walls that join the outhouses to the properties have been modelled with sloping tops: (A) back scene; (B) & (D) terraced rows modelled in 3mm scale; (C) cobbled street; (E) dividing walls with a sloping top to create the perspective linking the two scales together; (F) outhouses containing the toilets and coal stores, modelled in 4mm scale; (G) back alley to serve the terraced row; (H) stockade fence built with sleepers to form the perimeter to the railway; (I) double-tracked railway slightly raised on an embankment.

The urban landscape has again been modelled to perfection on this 1950s/60s model. The layout 'Leicester South' is the work of the Shipley Model Railway club. Note how the backs of the Victorian terraced houses back right up to the railway; a common sight in most of our industrial towns and cities, and well worth modelling.

Model of an industrial brewery branch. The railway tracks run into the brewery yards and even into some of the buildings, so all the buildings modelled here will have to be in the same scale as the railway. This layout plan is based on the breweries and malthouses formerly in Burton upon Trent: (A) malthouses and malthouse

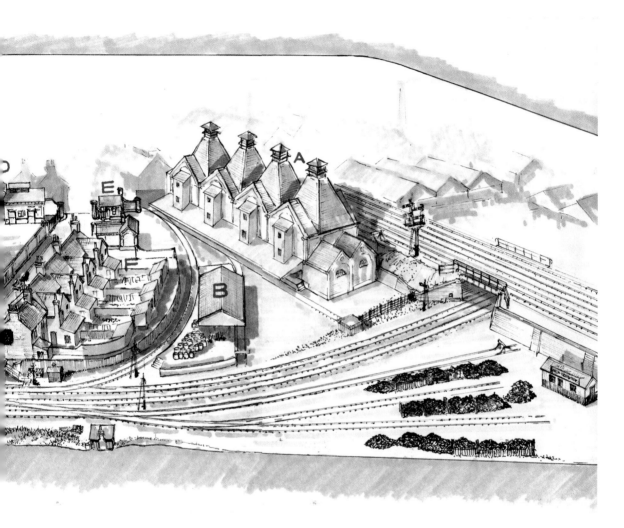

kilns; (B) ale docks, provided with canopies; (C) tower brewhouse; (D) brewery stables; (E) brewery gatehouses (F) terraced houses for brewery workers, with the local public house at the end of the terrace. Note the backyards and outhouses; (G) cooperage; (H) boundary fence made from sleepers and advertising hoadings.

CHAPTER FIVE

PAINTING AND WEATHERING

Achieving an authentic painted finish is the most important process in making models of urban buildings. Since this is the first thing that will be seen, if the finish is not applied correctly then the model will not look authentic, no matter how well the model is made. The processes are not difficult to apply but a little patience is needed to achieve reasonable results. Do not be tempted to rush this final process as this can spoil all your efforts. I use oil paints as a medium for all the painting processes as I find that every effect can be achieved with them. The paints are not expensive and you will require only about twelve tubes in total. All the other shades can be achieved by mixing the colours on a palette. I use the Winton range of oil paints produced by Windsor and Newton, although the Reeves Rowney range is just as good. There are also cheaper paints on the market produced in the Far East, although I would advise against using them as the results will not be as good.

PAINTING BUILDINGS WITH A STYRENE OR RESIN SKIN

The first painting process is to give the building a base colour. I strongly advise painting all the masonry before adding any windows and doors or fitting the roof to the building. The base colour is best achieved by using a spray paint, such as the Halfords acrylic range, that provides a close match to the masonry from which the building is built or faced. The Halfords Red Oxide primer spray, for example, is very good for replicating red brickwork. Always make sure that the spray paint chosen is matt rather than gloss, unless you are trying to achieve a glazed finish to the brickwork. Instead of sprayng, you can brush the paint on using Humbrol or other model paints, but again most applications will need the matt variety.

Once the base colour has been applied all over and has completely dried, the next stage is to add the mortar colour. For this I use oil paint, but in a thinned-down fashion. In order to match the mortar used, a light cream is usually mixed from a combination of Naples Yellow and Titanium White. The other common colour is a light grey mixed from Payne's Grey and Titanium White. Mix equal amounts of colour in a small tin or something similar. Do not be tempted to mix too much as it will only be wasted. Add turpentine thinners to this until you have a consistency of 30 per cent paint to 70 per cent thinners. When the mix is complete, brush this over the whole of the pre-painted masonry, letting the liquid run into all the mortar courses. The next stage is to remove the thinned-down paint from the surface of the masonry by rubbing it off with a dry tissue or paper towel, leaving the colour where you need it. You can also try dabbing the tissue or towel from time to time, which will give the effect of toning down the colour just a little. If you are attempting this on a large amount of brickwork, use a fresh tissue or towel frequently. Once you are happy with the result, put the model on one side to dry off completely.

DRY BRUSHING

With all the courses picked out, the next stage is to go over the face of the masonry adding all the tones to the brickwork. From your photographs of the chosen prototype you will see that most brick and stonework consists of a varying amount of tonal colour. The best way to achieve this effect on the model is to use the dry brushing technique. This requires using a paint mix that has been left to dry for a while, and sometimes removing paint from the brush before it is applied. The day before I need them for dry brushing, I squeeze the basic colours from the tubes of oil paint onto a palette. This way most of the oil will dry out, leaving just a dry pigment to work with. I would recommend using the earthy colours, such as Raw Umber, Burnt Umber, Yellow Ochre, Raw Sienna, Indian Red and Warm Red. You may also need colours to lighten (Naples Yellow and Titanium White) and darken (Payne's Grey and Lamp Black) the shades.

There is no need to purchase anything special to serve as a palette. I use plastic lids from ice cream tubs or biscuit cartons, for example, and anything similar will be fine, including video cassette cases.

Once the paints are laid out on the palette, start mixing the colours with a brush of reasonable size to replicate something close to the prototype. Don't be put off if you are not happy with the colour; just wipe it from the brush and try again. You will find that plenty of experimenting in mixing colours on the palette will help you become more experienced at achieving the correct colours. I always start with

The random colour tones to be found in brickwork.

Mix the mortar colour using equal amounts of Naples Yellow and Titanium White oil paint.

The next stage is to flood the mix with turpentine thinners to make a wash of paint.

The wash is now painted onto the embossed styrene sheet, making sure the colour floods into all the mortar joints.

The embossed styrene sheet should have an even coat of the wash all over.

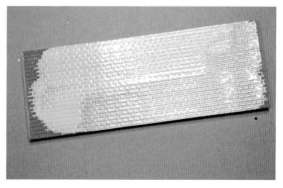

Excess paint can be removed from the face of the bricks using a soft tissue.

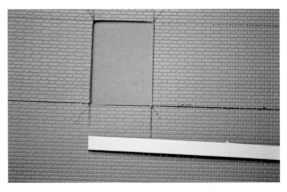

The sill and lintel for the window aperture are cut into a strip from card. Double-sided tape is used to make a neat fixing.

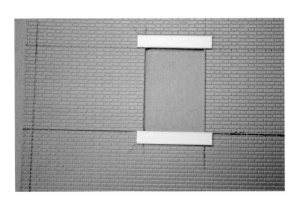

The sill and lintel fixed into position.

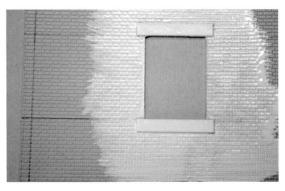

A wash of mortar colour is now applied to the section of brick walling containing the window.

Removing excess paint from the face of the brickwork, again using a tissue.

The finished result with the colour left in the mortar gaps.

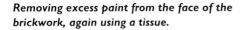

Colour variations within individual bricks. Also note the grey colour to the mortar.

Colour tones within a clinker wall. This material was used in towns that manufactured iron and steel, recycling the clinker waste from the industry.

the lighter shades of colour and then build them up with the darker shades. To apply the colour I use a 3mm (⅛ in) chisel brush, working across and down from the top left-hand corner with light strokes to create a random pattern. This technique will leave the paint on the surface of the masonry and it will not penetrate into pre-painted mortar courses. Repeat this technique with the darker shades. You might also wish to pick out a few bricks or stones in one colour, carefully painting them individually with a No. 1 brush.

Colour tones present within cobbles, paving bricks and kerbstones.

The last stage is to give a subtle blend of colours by going over the whole area with a very dry brush. You may need to add a darker grey shade to replicate the accumulations of dirt; this will apply especially to industrial and disused buildings. Weathering streaks should also be added where your photographs show that they appear on the prototype. You will see that darker streaks usually appear where rain running off guttering and sills penetrates the masonry. This

Detail of the colour and texture of peeling paint, exposing the brickwork underneath. Recreating this on a model can add extra character to a building.

The effects of decay are also visible here as render comes away from the brickwork.

especially applies to disused and derelict buildings where the guttering might be missing or downpipes have been broken. The lighter shades appear where the effect of the weather bleeds the mortar, creating whitish streaks. Again check your prototype for the subtle colour changes resulting from weathering.

Another weathering effect seen on walls and masonry, especially on buildings that are not maintained, is the natural growth of algae and lichens. Algae grows on damp walls and is seen on derelict buildings where missing guttering and downpipes have allowed water to penetrate the masonry. The easiest way of replicating this with paint is to first create a streak using a dark shade of grey. Go over this with a small amount of Sap Green or Lemon Yellow to create the colour. One way of making it look even more authentic is to brush some gloss

varnish over the top, creating a wet and slimy appearance.

With the main masonry completed, you may have to pick out the lintels or sills, especially if they are made from a different material. Stone ones are usually a buff shade that might weather to near black. Use shades of Naples Yellow, Titanium White and Yellow Ochre for these and darken as necessary with Payne's Grey.

PAINTING BUILDINGS WITH A DAS MODELLING CLAY SKIN

The technique used here is more or less the same, but there is no need to apply a base colour. The starting point here will be the addition of a wash of oil paint to create the mortar colour. The wash is mixed as described for use with a styrene or resin skin, but this time the liquid paint will penetrate into the material and capillary action takes it into the mortar courses that have been scribed in. The paint will be dry enough to work again after about one hour.

The next stage is to use the dry brushing technique as before, although more colour will have to be built up as no base colour was used. The blending and weathering process will also be the same, making sure that you replicate the tonal colour as accurately as you can. Always keep referring to photographs of the prototype at the painting stages.

PAINTING AND WEATHERING THE ROOF

In most cases, the preferred covering for urban buildings would be Welsh slate. Either card or styrene sheet may be selected to create the slate. A base coat of paint should first be applied. I use Humbrol Matt Tank Grey for this in spray form. This gives a flat colour, but photographs of the prototype will show that the slates are actually different shades. These can be created by mixing colours on the palette, starting with Payne's Grey and adding a little Mauve or Cobalt Blue. You can then use Titanium White and Naples Yellow to lighten the

The effect of weathering is clearly visible in the form of rusting on the roof of an industrial building. Although it is a challenge, a good representation of rust can be achieved by using a mix of Raw Sienna, Light Red and Chrome Orange.

A selection of colours demonstrating the shades that are often found in brickwork. When replicating the different shades present in the prototype, artists' oil paints usually give a better result.

Squeeze a little paint from the tubes onto a mixing palette.

Mixing can begin once all the colours are on the palette. I use an old video cassette case to mix on as it can be closed up when not in use, so avoiding any mishaps with wet paint.

The lighter shades are mixed first, using Light Red, Raw Sienna and Cadmium Orange, with a touch of Titanium White to lighten it.

Before applying the paint to the styrene sheet, try removing some of the paint with a tissue. The paint needs to be almost dry.

The paint is applied in light strokes across the raised surface of the brickwork.

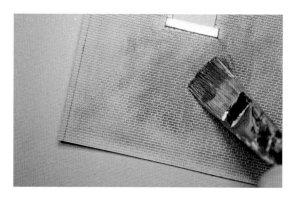

The darker shades can now be mixed and added to the surface in the same way.

Continue mixing darker shades using Raw Umber and Payne's Grey.

Always mix the shades on the palette in order to achieve the tonal variations found in the prototype brickwork.

Remove some of the paint from the brush as before.

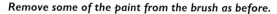

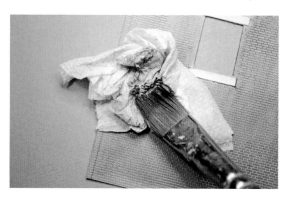

Weathering streaks are clearly visible where rain has run off the windowsill. This has been dry brushed on using the darker mix of paint.

The results of using the dry brushing technique on embossed brick styrene. Note that the sash window has now been fitted from the back to complete the effect.

shades or add more Payne's Grey to darken them. The technique is then to pick out slates in different shades in a random fashion. Once this has been completed, dry brush some Payne's Grey over to blend the shades together. To complete the roof, weathering is added by using Payne's Grey, applied by dry brushing from top to bottom in streaks to replicate the rain staining shown in the photographs. Where lead flashings are used on the roof, it is likely that rain has created a stain from these as well. It is probable

that this staining will appear light grey in colour, but you should check your prototype and try to replicate it using Titanium White with a little grey added. Other weathering on the roof may be the result of an accumulation of lichens and mosses growing on the ridges. Lichens and mosses will feature on any derelict building. To create the lichens on the model, I use a mix of Yellow Ochre with a tiny amount of Titanium White added. This is then stippled onto the roof using a No. 3 paintbrush, the bristles of which

Weathering effects, including rain staining, clearly visible on the two materials used to clad this industrial roof.

I have cut down to about half the original length, loading the brush with the paint nearly dry. As with all the other processes, consult your photographs to see just where they occur.

VEGETATION AND OTHER GROWTH

To complete this chapter it is worth examining the vegetation and growth that can establish itself on or beside urban buildings. This applies mainly to those that are disused and derelict, but it can soon take over occupied buildings if not kept in check. Buddleia, for example, can even establish itself into the mortar courses of most masonry. Grasses grow in blocked guttering, as can other plants such as silver birch saplings. Ivy and other creepers will cling to the sides of walls, and species such as rose-bay willowherb, bindweed and brambles will take over any available wasteland. It is not long before nature re-establishes itself, even in urban landscapes.

Various scenic materials can be used to create this vegetation and growth. For the grasses try using teddy bear fur, plumber's hemp or carpet underlay felt. You could also try using static grass in clump form. For ivy and other creepers use the foliage mattings produced by Heki, Woodland Scenics or Mini-Nature. Small saplings and buddleia bushes can be represented by using Noch Sea Moss or Sea Foam, which may be had from Gaugemaster. The flowers can be created by adding a little fine foam, which can be painted to replicate the petals. You can also try using some of the natural lichens, which can make very convincing plant life, although it may be worth spraying them with a matt fixative just to protect them. Always refer to photographs and take specific images of the plant life to use as reference. This way you will have a better chance of creating an authentic finish that looks convincing in miniature.

Rain staining on the wall of a derelict factory and the build-up of algae created by a broken downpipe.

The rain staining again running down the wall of this unmaintained building is the result of broken and missing guttering.

Rain staining and the build-up of algae close to pipework on the old mill. Note the different shades of green created by the weathered stone walls. Careful mixing of the paint and dry brushing should replicate this effect in miniature.

Weathering is again clearly visible on an old mill building in Belper.

The derelict railway warehouse in Derby clearly illustrates how nature soon starts to take over. The saplings that have managed to root themselves into the guttering and the edge of the roof can be replicated using small pieces of sea foam and foliage flock.

CHAPTER SIX

THE URBAN MODELLER'S SKETCHBOOK

In conclusion, here you will find what I have called 'The Urban Modeller's Sketchbook'. This is intended to give a quick visual reference to all the various techniques and materials that can be used in creating the architectural features of a vast array of urban buildings for use with model railways. I hope it will inspire you to create something special of your own. Happy Modelling!

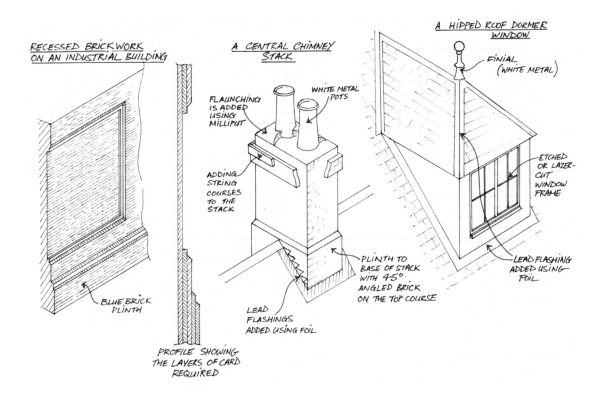

RECESSED BRICKWORK ON AN INDUSTRIAL BUILDING

BLUE BRICK PLINTH

PROFILE SHOWING THE LAYERS OF CARD REQUIRED

A CENTRAL CHIMNEY STACK

FLAUNCHING IS ADDED USING MILLIPUT

WHITE METAL POTS

ADDING STRING COURSES TO THE STACK

PLINTH TO BASE OF STACK WITH 45°. ANGLED BRICK ON THE TOP COURSE

LEAD FLASHINGS ADDED USING FOIL

A HIPPED ROOF DORMER WINDOW

FINIAL (WHITE METAL)

ETCHED OR LAZER-CUT WINDOW FRAME

LEAD FLASHING ADDED USING FOIL

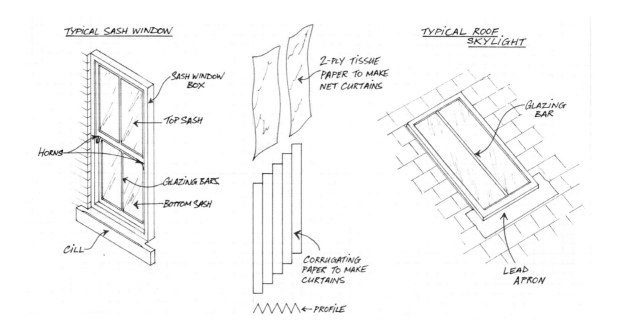

TYPICAL SASH WINDOW

SASH WINDOW BOX

TOP SASH

HORNS

GLAZING BARS

BOTTOM SASH

CILL

2-PLY TISSUE PAPER TO MAKE NET CURTAINS

CORRUGATING PAPER TO MAKE CURTAINS

MMMMM ← PROFILE

TYPICAL ROOF SKYLIGHT

GLAZING BAR

LEAD APRON

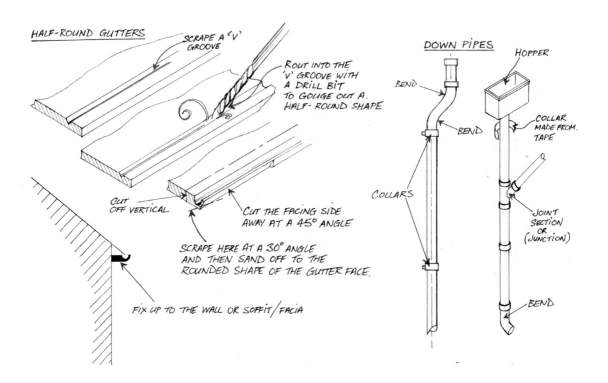

HALF-ROUND GUTTERS

SCRAPE A 'V' GROOVE

ROUT INTO THE 'V' GROOVE WITH A DRILL BIT TO GOUGE OUT A HALF-ROUND SHAPE

CUT OFF VERTICAL

CUT THE FACING SIDE AWAY AT A 45° ANGLE

SCRAPE HERE AT A 30° ANGLE AND THEN SAND OFF TO THE ROUNDED SHAPE OF THE GUTTER FACE.

FIX UP TO THE WALL OR SOFFIT/FACIA

DOWN PIPES

HOPPER

BEND

BEND

COLLARS

COLLAR MADE FROM TAPE

JOINT SECTION OR (JUNCTION)

BEND

SUPPLIERS OF EQUIPMENT, MATERIALS, KITS AND OFF-THE-SHELF MODELS

Scale rules, small squares, scalpels, blades, cutting mats, paintbrushes, dentist's probes and general tools

Squires Model and Craft Tools
100 London Road, Bognor Regis, West Sussex
PO21 1DD
Telephone: 01243 842424
www.squirestools.com

Eileen's Emporium
Unit 19.12, Highnam Business Centre, Newent Road, Gloucester GL2 8DN
Telephone: 01531 828009
www.eileensemporium.com

Hobby Holidays
The Spinney, Low Street, Beckingham, Doncaster
DN10 4PW
Telephone: 01427 848979
www.hobbyholidays.co.uk

Foam board, Das modelling clay, paints, brushes, styrene sheet and strip

Freestone Model Acessories
Newland Mill, Witney, Oxfordshire OX28 3HH
Telephone: 01993 775979
www.freestonemodel.co.uk

Slater's (Plastikard) Limited
Old Road, Darley Dale, Matlock, Derbyshire DE4 2ER
Telephone: 01629 734053
https://slatersplastikard.com

Evergreen Scale Models, Inc.
18620-F 141st Ave NE, Woodinville, WA 98072, USA
www.evergreenscalemodels.com
Scenic materials, accessories and dressings for buildings

Woodland Scenics
PO Box 98, Linn Creek, MO 65052, USA
www.woodlandscenics.com

Heki Kittler GmbH
Am Bahndamm 10, D-76437 Rastatt-Wintersdorf, Germany

Dart Castings
17 Hurst Close, Staplehurst, Tonbridge, Kent
TN12 0BX
Telephone: 01580 892917
www.dartcastings.co.uk

Langley Models
166, Three Bridges Road, Three Bridges, Crawley, West Sussex RH10 1LE
Telephone: 01293 516329
www.langleymodels.co.uk

Springside Models
2 Springside Cottages, Dornafield Road, Ipplepen, Newton Abbot, Devon TQ12 5SJ
Telephone: 01803 813749
www.springsidemodels.com

S&D Models
Highbridge Works, PO Box 101, Burnham-on-Sea, Somerset TA9 4WA
Telephone: 01278 781603
www.sanddmodels.co.uk

Duncan Models
34 Waters Road, Salisbury, Wiltshire SP1 3NX
Telephone: 01722 321041
www.duncanmodels.co.uk
Building kits, off-the-shelf models and accessories

Truetexture Ltd
13 The Priory, Middleton Street, Wymondham, Norfolk NR18 0AB
www.truetexture.co.uk

Superquick Model Kits
The Red House, Axminster, Devon EX13 5SE
Telephone: 01297 631435
www.superquick.co.uk

Metcalfe Models and Toys Ltd
Bell Busk, Skipton, North Yorkshire BD23 4DU
Telephone: 01729 830072
www.metcalfemodels.com

York Modelmaking and Display Ltd
Unit 13, The Bull Commercial Centre, Stockton-on-the-Forest, York YO32 9LE
Telephone: 01904 400358
www.yorkmodelmaking.co.uk

Skytrex Ltd
Unit 1, Charnwood Business Park, North Road, Loughborough, Leicestershire LE11 1LE
Telephone: 01509 213789
www.ogauge.co.uk

Scenecraft by Bachmann
Bachmann Europe Plc
www.bachmann.co.uk

Skaledale by Hornby
Hornby Hobbies Ltd, Westwood, Margate, Kent
CT9 4JX
www.hornby.com

Street scene accessories

Express Models
65 Conway Drive, Shepshed, Loughborough, Leicestershire LE12 9PP
Telephone: 01509 829008
www.expressmodels.co.uk

RMLectronics
1 Glebe Gardens, Beeford, East Riding of Yorkshire
YO25 8BF
Telephone: 01262 481264
www.rmlectronics.co.uk

DCCconcepts Pty Ltd
3/13 Lionel Street, Naval Base, WA 6165, Australia
www.dccconcepts.com

Tiny Signs
Available from www.gaugemaster.com

MUSEUMS AND INDUSTRIAL HERITAGE CENTRES OF INTEREST TO THE URBAN MODELLER

Finch Foundry
Sticklepath, Okehampton, Devon EX20 2NW
Telephone: 01837 840046
www.nationaltrust.org.uk/finch-foundry

Amberley Museum & Heritage Centre
Amberley, Houghton Bridge, Arundel, West Sussex
BN18 9LT
Telephone: 01798 831370
www.amberleymuseum.co.uk

Blists Hill Victorian Town
Ironbridge Gorge Museums, Telford, Shropshire
TF7 5DU
Telephone: 01952 433424
www.ironbridge.org.uk

Black Country Living Museum
Tipton Road, Dudley, West Midlands DY1 4SQ
Telephone: 0121 557 9643
www.bclm.co.uk

National Waterways Museum
South Pier Road, Ellesmere Port, Cheshire
CH65 4FW
Telephone: 0151 355 5017
http://canalrivertrust.org.uk/national-waterways-museum

Gloucester Waterways Museum
Llanthony Warehouse, The Docks, Gloucester
GL1 2EH
Telephone: 01452 318200
http://canalrivertrust.org.uk/gloucester-waterways-museum

Snibston Discovery Museum
Ashby Road, Coalville, Leicestershire LE67 3LN
Telephone: 01530 278444
www.leics.gov.uk

The Silk Mill
Derby Museums, Silk Mill Lane, Derby DE1 3AF
www.derbymuseums.org

St Fagans National History Museum
St Fagans, Cardiff CF5 6XB
Telephone: 029 2057 3500
www.museumwales.ac.uk

Kidwelly Industrial Museum
Broadford, Kidwelly, Carmarthenshire SA17 4LW
Telephone: 01554 891078
www.kidwellyindustrialmuseum.co.uk

Big Pit National Coal Museum
Blaenavon, Torfaen, NP4 9XP
Telephone: 029 2057 3650
www.museumwales.ac.uk

Cefn Coed Colliery Museum
Neath Road, Creunant, West Glamorgan SA10 8SN
Telephone: 01639 750556
www.npt.gov.uk

The Winding House
Cross Street, New Tredegar, Gwent NP24 6EG
Telephone: 01443 822666
www.caerphilly.gov.uk/windinghouse

National Slate Museum
Llanberis, Gwynedd LL55 4TY
Telephone: 029 2057 3700
www.museumwales.ac.uk

Astley Green Colliery Museum
Higher Green Lane, Astley Green, Tyldesley,
Manchester M29 7JB
Telephone: 01772 431937
www.agcm.org.uk

Beamish Museum
Beamish, County Durham DH9 0RG
Telephone: 0191 370 4000
www.beamish.org.uk

Crofton Beam Engines
Crofton Pumping Station, Crofton, Marlborough,
Wiltshire SN8 3DW
Telephone: 01672 870300
www.croftonbeamengines.org

Coldharbour Mill
Uffculme, Cullompton, Devon EX15 3EE
Telephone: 01884 840960
www.coldharbourmill.org.uk

Cauldwell's Mill
Bakewell Road, Rowsley, Matlock, Derbyshire
DE4 2EB
Telephone: 01629 734374
www.cauldwellsmill.co.uk

Etruria Industrial Museum
Lower Bedford Street, Etruria, Stoke-on-Trent
ST4 7AF
Telephone: 01782 233144
www.stoke.gov.uk

Cromford Mills
Mill Lane, Cromford, Matlock, Derbyshire DE4 3RQ
Telephone: 01629 823256
www.arkwrightsociety.org.uk/cromford-mills

Bellfoundry Museum
John Taylor & Co, Freehold Street, Loughborough,
Leicestershire LE11 1AR
Telephone: 01509 212241
www.taylorbells.co.uk

Helmshore Mills Textile Museum
Holcombe Road, Helmshore, Rossendale, Lancashire
BB4 4NP
Telephone: 01706 226459
www.lancashire.gov.uk

Port Sunlight Museum & Garden Village
23 King George's Drive, Port Sunlight, Wirral, CH62 5DX
Telephone: 0151 644 6466
www.portsunlightvillage.com

Quarry Bank Mill and Styal Estate
Quarry Bank Road, Styal, Wilmslow, Cheshire SK9 4LA
Telephone: 01625 527458
www.nationaltrust.org.uk

Queen Street Mill Textile Museum
Queen Street, Harle Syke, Burnley, Lancashire BB10 2HX
Telephone: 01282 412555
www.lancashire.gov.uk

Elsecar Heritage Centre
Wath Road, Elsecar, Barnsley, South Yorkshire S74 8HJ
Telephone: 01226 740203
www.elsecar-heritage-centre.co.uk

Leeds Industrial Museum at Armley Mills
Canal Road, Armley, Leeds LS12 2QF
Telephone: 0113 263 7861
www.leeds.gov.uk/armleymills

Bradford Industrial Museum
Moorside Mills, Moorside Road, Eccleshill, Bradford, West Yorkshire BD2 3HP
Telephone: 01274 435900
www.bradfordmuseums.org

Calderdale Industrial Museum (closed at time of writing)
Central Works, Square Road, Halifax, West Yorkshire HX1 0QG
Telephone: 01422 358087
www.calderdale.gov.uk

Abbeydale Industrial Hamlet
Abbeydale Road South, Sheffield, South Yorkshire S7 2QW
Telephone: 0114 272 2106
www.simt.co.uk

National Coal Mining Museum for England
Caphouse Colliery, New Road, Overton, Wakefield, West Yorkshire WF4 4RH
Telephone: 01924 848806
www.ncm.org.uk

Washington 'F' Pit Mining Museum
Albany Way, Washington, Tyne & Wear NE37 1BJ
Telephone: 0191 553 2323
www.twmuseums.org.uk

New Lanark World Heritage Village
New Lanark Mills, Lanark, Strathclyde, ML11 9DB
Tel: 01555 661345
www.newlanark.org

Bonawe Iron Furnace
Taynuilt, Argyll PA35 1JQ
Tel: 01866 822432
www.historic-scotland.gov.uk

National Mining Museum Scotland
Lady Victoria Colliery, Newtongrange, Midlothian EH22 4QN
Tel: 0131 663 7519
www.scottishminingmuseum.com

APPENDIX THREE

ORGANIZATIONS, SERVICES AND FURTHER INFORMATION

Gauge 0 Guild Limited
www.gauge0guild.com

English Heritage
www.english-heritage.org.uk

Dovedale Models (DVDs & Model Making Services)
David Wright, 6 Ivy Court, Hilton, Derbyshire DE65 5WD
Telephone: 01283 733547
www.dovedalemodels.co.uk

INDEX